Dear Viktor,

Be abundantly blessed!

Arnold Goetmyer

A Funny Thing Happened on the Way to the Pulpit

Arnold Lastinger

authorHOUSE®

AuthorHouse™
1663 Liberty Drive, Suite 200
Bloomington, IN 47403
www.authorhouse.com
Phone: 1-800-839-8640

© 2008 Arnold Lastinger. All rights reserved.

No part of this book may be reproduced, stored in a retrieval system, or transmitted by any means without the written permission of the author.

First published by AuthorHouse 6/5/2008

ISBN: 978-1-4343-8445-4 (sc)

Printed in the United States of America
Bloomington, Indiana

This book is printed on acid-free paper.

Contents

Chapter One	The Growing Up Years	1
Chapter Two	A Marriage Made In Heaven	11
Chapter Three	The Churches We Have Pastored	19
Chapter Four	Gainesville: We Almost Didn't Come!	39
Chapter Five	Cancer Evangelism	49
Chapter Six	A Felon In The Family	57
Chapter Seven	Tragedy Strikes The Lastingers	74
Chapter Eight	I Left Her Standing At The Station	79
Chapter Nine	Revival Fire In Gainesville	86
Chapter Ten	The Haiti Years	99
Chapter Eleven	A Romantic Night On The Terminal Floor	120
Chapter Twelve	Walking In The Footsteps Of Paul	130
Chapter Thirteen	The Closing Chapter	136

Foreward

I am a pastor—in much the same way that I am a man. It's the way God created me; it's both who I am and what I am. Different people have different ideas of what a pastor does. Some think he sleeps 'til noon each day; gets up and counts his money, and then goes back to take an afternoon nap. Kinder souls think he prays all night, studies all day and preaches on Sunday. But the truth is that he is just a man, not much unlike the men in your family. He faces the same troubles and trials that every other man faces. Sometimes he wins; sometimes he loses. That's life!

That's not to say, however, that a pastor does not have some unique experiences. That certainly seems to have been my lot in life. This book is a collection of just such experiences. I have written this book with only one goal in mind; I want to entertain you. I want you to enjoy reading these stories. I have purposely written them in a Reader's Digest style so that you can read a single chapter at one sitting. Some of the chapters will leave you laughing; some will make you cry. Others will cause you to rejoice in the greatness of our God. Some may even serve as a teaching device for you and open your eyes to something you had not thought about before. Some of the stories may seem so absurd as to be untrue; but, I assure you that every story in this book is true and has not been embellished in any way. Sometimes I may have changed some names so as not to embarrass the people involved, but the facts are true in every case.

The book you are about to read was written over several years. In a flash of inspiration I would write a chapter and then stop. Sometimes a year would pass before I felt the next flash of inspiration. And then, I would write some more. The miscellaneous stories you will read here happened over the span of a lifetime. I never intended however, to write an autobiography. Most of our lives are lived at a rather mundane pace during which time nothing really interesting takes place. Most biographies fail because they try to take uninteresting things and make them interesting reading—an impossible task! I hope that does not happen in this book.

What I have attempted to do is to take some of the interesting times in our family's lives and string them together in a more-or-less chronological sequence. I guess, by definition that makes this an autobiography, but that is not my intent. Many important things have been left out of this book; because of that, it may appear at times to be disjointed. Having been a "once upon a time" English teacher, I cringe at some of the grammatical mistakes in the book. But, that's the way we Americans talk; and, I wanted to be real and readable. No apologies; I did not start out to write an academically perfect book. Remember, I just want to entertain you.

My greatest joy has always been to preach God's Word. I am a total stranger to the fear some people have when called upon to stand behind the sacred desk. My week is filled with anticipation along the path to the pulpit. But, some interesting things have happened along that path. Please enjoy *A Funny Thing Happened on the Way to the Pulpit*.

Arnold L. Lastinger

Chapter One
The Growing Up Years

Remember *Ozzie & Harriet* and *Leave it to Beaver*? When Dad came to dinner in a suit and tie, and Mom served dinner looking like she had just stepped out of the pages of Vogue magazine? A time when every crisis had a happy ending and usually was resolved within thirty minutes? Well, let's just say, that doesn't describe my childhood.

The truth is that both of my parents were drunks. They were hard-drinking party animals who couldn't live with each other and couldn't live without each other. They finally parted ways and divorced before I ever started to school, but not before I had two little sisters, Delana and Judy. Mom and Dad both remarried again not too long afterward, and, true to form, they both married drunks the second time around. Now I had four drunks for parents! Lucky me! My mother bore two sons by her second husband before he was killed in a drunken, head-on collision just outside Sumter, South Carolina in 1951.

My mother remained single for a short time and I remember several men that she was romantically involved with during that time. However, my most vivid memory was of a business venture she entered into in the town of Conway, South Carolina. To all outward appearances, it looked like an innocent gasoline service station on the main street of the city. However, what went on behind closed doors staggers the imagination! I was too young to understand the business end of what was going on, but I remember that a lot of couples disappeared into the bedrooms for an hour or two before going on their merry way! I remember one night in particular when the police showed up with a warrant to search our premises. I was amused to watch the naked bodies jumping out the windows with clothing in hand, only to disappear into the darkness! They must have all gotten away because I don't remember that Mom ever spent a night in jail over the incident.

MY SEX EDUCATION?

I'm sure you have figured out by now that I had no Christian influence in my childhood. At this point in time, I was 12 years old and I knew little to nothing about sex. I had figured out that this was the way to have babies, and I assumed that it must be fun because everybody seemed to be doing it. One of my mom's boyfriends had a 14-year old daughter named Shelby Jean. She led me to believe that she had a world of experience in this mysterious field, and that she would be happy to teach me everything I needed to know about the subject. Do I need to tell you that I was a willing learner?

Conway, S.C. is in the middle of the tobacco belt, and one day found Shelby Jean and me working together in the tobacco fields. Making sure that no one was looking; she took me by the hand and led me away at lunch time to give me my first lesson. We found an old, one-holer outhouse and had just settled down for my first lesson in human anatomy. Just as things were about to get interesting, we heard the voice of her father shouting, "Shelby Jean, where are you? You come out here girl!" I don't know whether it was the August heat in that old outhouse or the fear in my gut, but great drops of sweat flowed down my 12-year old face. Shelby Jean and I made a date to meet later in the week to finish my introduction to sex education and she hastily exited the outhouse with some lame excuse about having to go to the bathroom. Amazingly, her father bought it and she went back to the barn with him. I waited for what seemed like an eternity before rejoining the workers at the tobacco barn. Throughout the afternoon, trying not to be noticed, Shelby Jean and I cast furtive glances at each other, waiting for our date later in the week.

That night, my mother announced that we were moving to Jacksonville, Florida the next day. I never saw Shelby Jean again. I didn't know it then, but God had preserved my virginity so that I could give it to the woman who has shared my life for the last half century.

THE POKER PLAYING ADOLESCENT

Our stay in Jacksonville did not last long however. My mother had met a man in South Carolina who was to become her third husband. Not surprisingly, he also was a drunk. Not too long afterward, they were married and we moved to Aynor, S.C. to operate a Shell service station. The station was in a remote farming area at a crossroads in what could best be described as "the boonies." In those days, it was not uncommon for families to live on the premises of the business they operated. The service station comprised most of the ground floor except for the kitchen which was directly behind the inside counter of the station. Stairs led upstairs to the living area that we called home.

In my 13th year, my mom and step-dad decided to take a weekend off and go see his family across the state. They left me to run the business. I was a mixture of emotions. I was proud that they had confidence that I could handle that adult responsibility. But, it is hard to say which was bigger, my false sense of bravado that I could handle the job, or my overwhelming sense of fear that something would come up that I could not handle. I did alright during the day, but when night came my fears rose to the surface. A number of older guys had gathered to play penny poker, and I happily joined them. As midnight neared, I knew I should send them home, but their presence was comforting to me, so I let them stay. Daybreak found us still playing poker. The gang finally disbanded to get some sleep and I kept the station open for business.

Sunday afternoon, my mom and step-dad came home drunk and arguing very loudly. Disgusted by their drunkenness and exhausted from a night of poker, I went upstairs to go to bed. In a few minutes, my sister Delana came running up the stairs screaming,

"He's beating her! He's beating her!"

I angrily pulled on my pants and went running down the stairs, cursing him for everything I could think of. The two of them were struggling in the confined area behind the counter. He had an electric extension cord in hand and was beating my mother with it. She was trapped behind the dead-end counter and could not get out. I had already used up my entire vocabulary of curse words, so I ran into the kitchen and got the largest butcher knife I could find. I came up behind him and called his name. With bloodshot eyes, he turned toward me.

"If you hit her one more time," I said, mustering all the courage that a 12-year old boy is capable of, "I will cut your heart out and lay it here on this counter!" Through bleary eyes, he looked at me for a moment, and then correctly concluded that I was bluffing. He lunged at me with the extension cord. Not wanting to kill him, I stabbed the knife into the countertop and turned to run out the door into the fading sunlight. I heard his shouts as I ran down the dirt road,

"If you ever come back, I'll cut you to ribbons."

I muttered under my breath, "Don't worry Buster, you'll never have that chance!" I finally came to the farmhouse of a friend and asked if I could spend the night. His father agreed. We had supper and went to bed.

The next morning after breakfast, I assumed that my stepfather would be sleeping off a huge hangover and that he wouldn't even remember what had happened the night before. As I approached the station, however, I was surprised to see him crossing the road to put something in the mailbox. He paused for a moment, looked down the road to where I was walking, then turned and went back into the station. Since he had showed no emotion, I assumed that he had forgotten all about the night before. Lesson: never assume anything!

Wordlessly, I followed him into the station and made my way around the counter to the barstool where I usually sat, acting as though everything was normal. I opened a comic book and began to read. An ominous shadow fell across the page of the comic book. I turned to see him standing, extension cord in hand, blocking the only exit from the counter where I was sitting. With a low, growling voice, he said,

"I told you that if you ever came back I would cut you to ribbons; now, I'm going to do it!" My only way of escape was to get by him, or over the counter. Even if I jumped over the counter, the exit door beside the counter was locked. He would get me before I could get out. I was trapped! Luckily, my mother was making breakfast in the kitchen behind the counter and heard his growling voice. Just as he was raising the extension cord for his first blow, Mom grabbed the cord from behind his back. Taken by surprise, he turned toward her. I took advantage of the situation to jump over the counter in order to escape. He pushed Mom down on the floor and ran around the end of the counter; he had me trapped again! My only way of escape was to run beside him for the main exit doors behind him. But, he was too fast for that; I would never make it. I was doomed! Again, just as he was raising the extension cord for his first blow, Mom grabbed it again from behind him. Distracted, he turned toward her and pushed her away. I took advantage of his distraction to run by him toward the front door. Unfortunately, I tripped over the threshold and fell to the gravel drive outside the front door of the station. I was falling face down and all I could think of was that he would slice my back open with that extension cord. I twisted my body as I fell so that I would land on my back. I hoped to fight off the dreaded extension cord with my hands. He managed to get in one blow before I got to my feet. Making sure that I was safely outside his reach, I paused just long enough to once again exhaust my entire vocabulary of curse words on him before I left, vowing never to return again.

I made my way back to the same farmhouse where I had spent the previous night. I explained the situation to the farmer and asked if I could live there with him and work for my keep. He agreed and his son and I headed for the barn where our assignment for the day was to shell corn. We worked until midday when I heard a car outside the barn. I went out to find my mother sitting in the car.

"Get in, Son!" she said.

"Never, Mom; I'm never going home to any house that man is in," I said.

"He and I have talked," she said, "He has agreed to give me sole responsibility for you. He'll never give you another order; you'll have no more trouble from him."

She finally convinced me and I got in the car and went home with her. For the next year, we lived in the same house, but he and I never spoke a word to each other!

Over the years, however, that relationship has healed. As of this writing, he is in his 90's and is in frail health. We are friends and he tells me that he has made his peace with God. Fifty years after the above events took place I was thanking him for being a father to us kids and being willing to adopt a ready-made family. His face clouded up and he said,

"There are some things I wish I could go back and do differently!"

"Don't we all, Troy! Don't we all!" I said.

Not long afterward, my Mom called me upstairs to show me something. She pulled out a wad of bills and counted out forty $100 bills. I had never seen so much money in my life! They had sold the service station and we were moving to Jacksonville.

AND THEN I MET JESUS!

They bought a house in the Westconnett area of Jacksonville, not too far from my grandparent's home. The first thing that I noticed was that my grandmother had changed! She wasn't the same woman I had known before. Something had happened to that switch-wielding, sharp-tongued, cursing witch I had known before. Someone had kidnapped her and substituted a sweet, loving, hymn-singing grandma in her place. I was entranced with this new grandma. When she invited me to go to church with her, I was definitely interested. I wanted to see what could make this kind of change in a woman like her. Saintly she may have been; naïve she was not. Granny knew exactly what would capture the heart of a 14-year old boy. "I want you to drive me to church, Son!" she said. Now, what 14-year old boy wouldn't jump at any chance to get to drive?

What little religious experience I had been exposed to did not prepare me for what I saw that first Sunday. Those people sang with such joy and enthusiasm that it surprised me. And, they even clapped their hands or raised them toward the ceiling. Some were even speaking in a strange language. It's not that they were all that wild or fanatical; it's just that this was a far cry from what I had experienced in the few other churches I had visited in my childhood. As I was driving my grandmother home that day I said,

"Granny, I'll go to that church with you every week. But, I want you to know that the only reason I'm going is because you let me drive your car. But, if you think I'm ever gonna become one of those 'holy rollers' you can think again. That's just not gonna happen!"

Granny smiled sweetly with a knowing gleam in her eye and said, "OK, son."

The next Sunday came and I chauffeured Granny to Riverside Assembly of God in Jacksonville. Granny believed in "sitting close to the fire" so we ended up sitting on the second row from the front. The service progressed about like it had the week before, but I had grown accustomed to the noisy worship atmosphere. Then, when the pastor got up to preach, things really began to happen. It seemed like he named off every sin I had ever committed. It was like he had followed me around for the last year or two and made notes on all my activities. I just knew that Granny had called him that week and told him all about me. Then I realized that not even Granny knew all those things he was telling. Then, he started talking about hell and how people like me were going to go there because of all our sins. By the time he gave his altar call, I was literally shaking in my seat and tears were running down my cheeks. Granny said nothing; she just took me by the elbow and gave me a gentle push toward the altar. That's all I needed. The next thing I knew, I found myself draped across the altar bench, my tears pooling on the concrete floor. The last thing any 14-year old boy wants is for people to see him cry; but, at that point I didn't really care. I was overcome with sorrow for my sins and fearful of having to spend eternity in hell. I know that "hell fire and brimstone" preaching is not the best way to get people to Jesus, but I'll have to say that it sure worked in my case.

To this day I don't know who they were, but two little white-haired ladies met this teenager at the altar with their Bibles open. In the next few minutes they showed me that God really loved me and that Jesus had paid the penalty for my sins so that I would not have to go to that hell I was so terrified of. Then, they showed me what I had to do to accept the sacrifice that Jesus had made for me. They prayed with me and I invited Jesus to come into my heart and be Lord of my life. When I got up from the altar I knew that I had been forgiven and that hell was not a part of my future. I felt as if I floated back to my seat. That night, I slept peacefully with no fear of the future.

Ironically, Riverside was an affluent church located in an aristocratic part of the city. On the other hand, I was a kid from the other side of the tracks, brought up in a near-poverty lifestyle. I even remember living in an old Army surplus canvas tent with a dirt floor and rotting holes in the top of the tent. We had to be careful where we put our beds so that rain would not drip on it through the holes. I would wake up in the morning to see my mother cooking breakfast on a two-burner porcelain kerosene stove. What kind of reception would this kid from the back side of the tracks receive from this affluent, uptown church? The fact is that the whole church adopted me and surrounded me with love. For the first time in my life I felt loved; I felt as if I belonged. I had a family.

A few weeks later, on a Sunday afternoon after church, a friend and I carved a couple of tiny boats out of balsa wood. Even though it was raining we decided to go down to a small creek to float our boats. Mom had given her permission for us to go. We had only gone about a block from the house when my little brother came running after us, wanting to tag along.

"No," I said, "not without Mama's permission!"

"But, she told me I could come!" he lied.

"OK, come on," I reluctantly said, and off we went to the creek. A little while later Mom's car drove up and she began to rail on me for allowing Kenny to come along. She was deaf to my protest that Kenny had told me he had permission to come. She ordered me home immediately then drove off to the errand she had been headed to before she came by. My punishment for that offense was that I would not be allowed to go to church anymore. Later that afternoon, Granny came by to pick me up for church.

"I can't go, Granny, Mama won't let me," I said tearfully.

"Dell, what's gotten into you?" Granny said to my mother who had followed me out of the house into the yard.

"What makes him think he can take MY SON out into the rain like that without my permission?" she yelled at Granny. The words cut into my heart like a knife. "My son," she had said; and she wasn't talking about me! So, where did that leave me? Was I just some unwanted boarder in her house? I ran inside, threw my clothes into a paper sack, and came back outside to Granny's car. I got in and rode off to church, never to return home again. At age 14, I went to live with Granny and Grandpa Shreve.

Strangely however, my relationship with my mom and step-dad was not antagonistic. We saw each other occasionally and our conversations were always cordial, almost as if nothing had happened; I just wasn't living at home anymore. I lived with Grandpa and Granny until I fell in love with a little redhead named Joy Clark. She lived all the way across Jacksonville, an hour away, and went to a different school. So I moved across town to live with my dad whose house was in the same school district as Joy's. I lived there until I went away to Bible College in the fall of 1956.

LIFE WITH DAD AND BILLIE

My life in my daddy's home was a lonely existence. His wife, Billie, was unable to have children, so they were childless. She made no secret of the fact that she resented Dad's three children, and she would not allow him to show us any affection at all. I never felt that their house was my home; I was simply a guest who was allowed to stay there. There were never any angry words, however; they weren't home enough to have any words with. Every night was spent in a local "juke joint" that they frequented; one of those places "where everybody knows your name." They would go there straight from work and not get home until 11:00 at night, often so drunk that they could not walk straight. Sometimes they would get into arguments at the bar and he would leave her sitting there. Several times from my bedroom I would hear noises from the back porch. I would find him passed out in the floor, unable to make it into the house. I don't know how he drove home without killing himself or some unfortunate person who happened to get in his way. I would drag him into his bedroom, undress him and put him to bed. A little while later a taxi would drive up and Billie would stagger into the house and climb into bed with him. The next day they would get up and go to work as if nothing had happened. Such was life in the Lastinger house; a lonely existence for a 16-year old boy. If it had not been for my church family, it would have been a desolate time in my life.

I passed a major milestone in life while I was with Dad and Billie; I got my driver's license! There were few 2-car families in those days, and a teenager with a car was a real rarity. Nevertheless, I approached my dad about allowing me to use the car.

"If you'll just let me have the car for Sundays and Wednesdays, and one night a month for youth rallies, I won't ask for it any other time," I promised.

Sundays were no problem; the bar wasn't open then. Wednesdays were quite a sacrifice for Dad and Billie. That night they did their drinking at home! Dad only issued one warning concerning the car. "Boy, you better have that car home in time for me to go to work tomorrow!" he said. Most teenagers would have seen such lack of restraint as freedom; I saw it as a lack of love. The car arrangement lasted until I bought my own car in my senior year in high school. Dad and Billie continued their nightly beer-drinking escapades until…but that's another chapter!

Chapter Two
A Marriage Made In Heaven

"Arnold & Joy Lastinger, 1956"

    I accepted the Lord Jesus as my Savior in September, 1953 and I instantly fell deeply in love with Him. Oh, I had a lot of things in my life that needed cleaning up and straightening out, but I was passionately in love with Jesus and I never doubted His love for me.

A Funny Thing Happened on the Way to the Pulpit

Finding a girl friend was not my highest priority at that time. But that was about to change!

I arrived late for church one Sunday and had to browse around for a seat. The only one I could find available placed me beside a beautiful, young reddish-blonde girl and her overly-protective mother. In the months since I had been saved, I don't know why I had not noticed this girl, but this was the first time I remembered meeting her. I don't remember anything our pastor preached about that day, but I sure do remember that girl!

Joy and I started dating far too young (we were both 14 years old.) Most of our dates were either chaperoned by her older brother or in the company of the rest of the church youth group. Our first date, however, was to a football game at the Gator Bowl in Jacksonville, Florida. At 14 I was much too young to drive, so my father had to take us to the game and pick us up afterward. I was trying my best to make a good impression on this cute little strawberry blonde that I was with; I really wanted her to like me! At the game we met one of my friends who shouted across the stands, "Hey, Arnold; who's that? She's not the chick you were with last week!" What really made matters worse is that he was right! I mumbled a few words trying to excuse my friend and escorted my date up into the stands. I don't even remember who the two teams were that were playing, but it didn't matter; I was the real winner that night! I didn't know it then, but I had found my future wife.

I don't think we could say that it was love at first sight. Instead, our romance blossomed slowly and smoothly over the next 4 years. Neither of us was the kind to date around. We both tended to make commitments and stick with them. Neither of us ever seriously considered anyone else after our first date. I tend to act decisively and make decisions quickly, so I knew she was the one for me right away. Joy, on the other hand, is more deliberate and gathers tons of information before making a decision. It took me three years to convince her that she loved me. Although we had talked about marriage, nothing official had ever been agreed upon. On the night of her high school graduation in June, 1957, I asked her to be my wife and presented her with an engagement ring. Holding the ring in her hand, she had to make a decision—did she love me enough to become my wife? Thankfully, she heard from God and said "Yes!"

By the grace of God, Joy and I remained virgins through our courtship. However, I can take no credit for that; I tried every trick I knew, but fortunately, Joy knew how to say "No!" In my defense, I had no moral compass to guide me during my growing-up years. There were no parents who cared enough, or whose own standards were high enough to set any boundaries for me. I honestly did not know how to avoid sexual temptations. One of the great paradoxes that I discovered is that a person can love God with all his heart and still be no match for the hormones raging within him. The only solution is to "flee youthful lusts" as the Apostle Paul advised his young protégé in 2 Timothy 2:22. My problem was that I had not discovered that scripture at that time.

Joy's sex education also left much to be desired. The only conversation she ever had was with her mother on the day she started her first menstrual period. Terrified that she was going to die, she confided in her mother what had happened. "Don't worry about it, Joy; it will happen once a month from now on" was all she was told. The rest of her sex education she got from the Marriage and Family textbooks I brought home from college in my first two years. Fortunately for both of us, however, Joy had been saved at age five and had a much stronger moral backbone than I had by her teenage years. As a result, we both were able to bring the gift of virginity to our marriage bed in 1958, a treasure that both of us have cherished for half a century.

An interesting and humorous side note to the above story is that my younger sister began to go along with us on our chaperoned dates to make up the foursome. She fell in love with Joy's brother and they ended up getting married a year before we did! The week after their honeymoon, I picked Joy up for a date. When she got in the car, she was wide-eyed. I thought I heard her say excitedly,

"Guess what; they made it!"

"What do you mean, 'they made it'" I asked?

After several exchanges, I figured out that she was actually saying, "They mated!" I snickered and said,

"Well, so what? They're married now, it's OK!" Horrified, she looked at me and said,

"But, on the first night? Shouldn't they have waited a little while?" I laughed and took her hand in mine;

"I sure hope you change your mind before next June!" I said, as we drove off on our date.

On June 2, 1958 Joy and I were married. Eight days later, I turned 19 years old. I had just finished my second year of Bible College at Southeastern Bible College (now Southeastern University) in Lakeland, Florida. I had no money, no job and no shoes to get married in. I borrowed $5 from my dad to buy a pair of black shoes on my wedding day. Joy was a telephone operator and had already paid for the rent on our apartment, the deposits on all the utilities, and the down payment on our car. Not a very promising beginning for what has turned into a wonderful marriage.

With the exception of one uncle, every person on both sides of my family had been divorced and remarried at least once. One aunt had been married eleven times! Once she even stole her own sister's husband and married him! I had lived through a broken home and seen enough divorces that I never wanted to see another. On our wedding night, the first order of business for Joy and me was to kneel beside our bed and covenant together that the word "divorce" would never be spoken in our home. In fifty years neither of us has ever considered divorce (murder a few times, but never divorce!)

The dysfunctional family background that I came from took its toll on our married life for the first twelve years. I had no role model for a Christian husband or father. I barked orders and expected instant obedience from wife and child alike. I considered displays of affection as un-manly. I thought I was being noble and self-sacrificing when I placed my ministry above my family in my priorities. I know now that it was not nobility—it was stupidity! The deepest regret of my life is that I deprived myself and my children of the affection they needed during their growing up years. I never attended a Little League game or a PTA meeting. I never tussled with them in the floor or played football with them. I wish I could go back and recover that.

Fortunately, that all began to change in 1970. I enrolled in a CPE class (Clinical Pastoral Education) at Georgia Southwestern State Hospital in Thomasville, Georgia to learn how to become a pastoral counselor and help people with their problems. It wasn't long until I began to recognize some of those problems in my own life and marriage. It didn't take much intelligence to realize that I would never be able to help other people with their problems until I had come to grips with my own. I made a conscious decision that, with God's help, I would learn how to be a godly husband and father. It was not an overnight process, but the change began in that year and I am still learning. By the grace of God, I was able to salvage a good relationship with my five sons and we love each other very much to this very day. In the process I discovered that it was much more fun being married to a woman with her own mind than to a robot that did everything I commanded her to do.

THE EARLY YEARS

After our wedding, I took a job with Tooley-Myron Studios as a professional portrait photographer. I got the job on grit alone because I surely did not have the qualifications. My intentions were to work for a year to earn enough money to pay off my school bill and then go back and finish college. Two things happened to change those plans. The federal government began giving student loans to college students and another photographer convinced my boss that he could take better pictures than I could (he could!) With my "pink slip" in hand, I decided to go back to Southeastern. Shortly after reporting for school, we discovered that Joy was pregnant with our first child. It might have been good news, except that she had morning sickness 24 hours a day, seven days a week for 9 straight months! To make matters worse, I was in school from 7:30 a.m. to 1:00 p.m. and worked seven days a week from 11:00 p.m. to 7:00 a.m. cleaning the Kraft foods citrus processing plant in Lakeland, Florida. I had no time to help her at home, and I felt so guilty leaving her throwing up when I went to school and when I went to work. At the end of the first semester, we decided to go home so I would have more time to be able to help her.

I took a job at May Company in Jacksonville selling carpets to make ends meet. Imagine my surprise when the owner of the Tooley-Myron chain appeared on my sales floor. "Would you be willing to go back to work for me as a portrait photographer if I sent you to Miami for training?" he asked. I loved photography and it didn't take me long to make up my mind. In a few days I was on a train to Miami where I spent two weeks training under one of America's best portrait photographers. He gave me the professional skills that I had previously lacked. I worked for Tooley-Myron for a year before opening up my own studio in Orange Park, Florida. Business was good and we shortly opened up another studio in Lake Shore, a suburb of Jacksonville.

Two major mistakes marred my time in Orange Park. The first mistake I made was in not paying my tithes. I rationalized my failure to do so by telling God that I was giving Him my whole life, so what's 10%? (I was starting a home mission church in Orange Park at the time.) One thing I have discovered is that you can never win an argument with God. Human logic is beneath Him.

The second mistake was to enter into a business partnership with an unsaved man. He was knowledgeable in the sales end of the portrait business and I thought I really needed him. It seemed to be a good working arrangement; I would do all the photography and finishing work and he would take care of sales. We were doing a lot of business, but never seemed to have any money to spend. I discovered too late that he was pocketing money from sales that I never saw. In 1960 our family survived all year on $34 per week! But, God could not bless us financially because we were living in disobedience to His Word. I finally sold my share of the business and we headed back to Bible College with three little boys in tow!

I wanted to get finished with my degree program as quickly as possible, so I registered for 21 credit hours per semester, hoping to finish two years in 3 semesters. I got a really good, white-collar job as night auditor for the Holiday Inn in Lakeland. I worked the graveyard shift from 11 to 7, seven days a week for over a year without a day off. My take-home pay was $52 per week! Joy enrolled the children in day-care and went to work as a waitress at Woolworth's soda fountain in south Lakeland. Our daily routine was hectic to say the least. I would come home from work at 7:00 a.m. in time to take the children to day care and then go to class. I would get out of class at 1:00 and study in the library until about 4:00. I would pick her up from work and then come home to go to bed. She would awaken me at 10:00 to feed me and get me off to work. Joy was a godsend to me that year. I would dictate my papers to her on Saturday morning before I went to bed. She would take them down in shorthand and then type them up for me to proofread when I awakened. She would type the final draft on Sunday afternoon and I would turn in my assignments on Monday morning. I never could have made it without her.

I was allowed to march through the graduation line in May of 1962 but I did not actually finish my classes until the end of summer school. I began to make some calls about churches that may be looking for a pastor. (Résumés were unheard of in the ministry at that time!) Nothing opened up and I began to get quite discouraged. I was still working for the Holiday Inn at the time and that kept our heads above water financially. One day while I was praying I heard the Lord tell me, "You're depending on the Holiday Inn; I want you to depend on me. Turn in your resignation and trust me!" I would never give that advice to anyone else, but I felt so strongly that it was God that I did not even hesitate. The next day, I had breakfast with my boss and told of him of my decision.

"Stay with me, Arnold, and I will send you to management training school and get you an Inn of your own!" he said.

"That's tempting, Mr. Spicer" I told him, "but God didn't call me to be an innkeeper—He called me to preach the gospel!" He looked at me and smiled.

"I figured you would probably say that" he said. I obeyed God, turned in my resignation, and in a few days I was pastoring in Mobile, Alabama. But, that's another chapter.

"Our Family in Mobile, Alabama; 1962"
l-r David, Arnold, Allen, Joy, Steven; back row Ron Haltiwanger, Arnold's brother)

Chapter Three
The Churches We Have Pastored

Almost immediately after I got saved I knew I would one day be in ministry. I'm not exactly sure how that idea even came into my mind. There was no dramatic, Damascus Road experience, no fiery finger writing on the wall, and no booming voice from heaven mandating that I should "Preach Christ." It was more like a growing awareness that this was to be my destiny. No doubt, I was influenced by the pastors I idolized. The man under whose ministry I was saved, Roy Harthern, was a handsome young Brit with a captivating accent and an intoxicating smile. On top of that, he was a powerful pulpiteer. I wanted very much to be a powerful preacher like him. But, the man who probably influenced me the most was my second pastor, Lyman B. Richardson. Although not the pulpiteer that Harthern was, Pastor Richardson was the gentle, loving, father figure that I had never known. His son, Bill and I were best friends. I would often go home with them on Sunday after church and I would overhear as Brother Richardson would answer the telephone, "Pastor Richardson; how can I help you?" I knew that I wanted to be that kind of man; I wanted to help people.

I don't want to leave you with the idea that becoming a minister of the gospel was all my idea. Although I did not understand the process, God was calling me into the ministry as a teenager. What started out as a nice idea, became a growing awareness that this was my calling in life. There was nothing else that even appealed to me. As my teen years flew by, that growing awareness became a driving compulsion; there simply was no other choice for me. The die was cast; my destiny was determined. A preacher of the Gospel I would be!

After my graduation from high school, I wanted to go to Bible College. In my non-Christian family, however, there was no money for such frivolities. If I was going to Bible College I would have to do it on my own. I postponed the idea in my mind and decided to get a job, save up the money and go later. Pastor Richardson came to me one day and said,

"Arnold, I understand that you want to go to Bible College to prepare for ministry."

"Yes, sir," I said, "but I can't afford it right now; I'm going to have to get a job first."

"If you really want to go," he said, "I don't want you to put it off. If you will go ahead and send your application, the church will help you." My heart jumped up in my throat. I had visions of a monthly check coming to me to pay my school expenses for the next four years. A few weeks later, I left for Bible College with the church's check for $100 in my hand. It was the only money I would ever receive from the church! But, no matter, God had accomplished His purpose; I was a student at Southeastern Bible College in Lakeland, Florida.

In those days, there was no financial aid for college students. The federal and state governments had not yet developed their systems for assisting needy college students. Unless you had a scholarship (non-existent in Bible Colleges) you paid your own way or lived a precarious life of faith trusting God to bring in the funds as the need arose. Since I had no money and no other financial resources, I was forced to take the faith path. Miraculously, I graduated from Southeastern six years later owing them just $700!

Joy's nine-month bout with morning sickness cut short our third year at Southeastern. We dropped out of school and moved back home to Jacksonville so I would have more time to help her through her first pregnancy.

ORANGE PARK, FLORIDA

My passion for ministry had not diminished, however. I lived in southwest Jacksonville and there was no Assembly of God church anywhere nearby. I arbitrarily selected the sleepy little bedroom community of Orange Park as a great place to plant a church. There was no A/G church meeting there, no nucleus of people to start with, and no money for the project. What we did have was a small, residential lot that had been donated by some anonymous donor for the purpose of building a church in Orange Park. The lot was far too small and in the wrong area of town to build a church. With the district's approval, we sold the lot for $700 and purchased a low-land lot about two miles outside of town on Kingsley Ave. The property was so low that water stood in the lot when it rained. I contacted the city and county governments and asked them to bring me all the clean landfill they could to fill in the lot. I spent many hours with a shovel in the hot, Florida sunshine spreading that dirt and leveling the ground to get it ready for building.

On one end of the lot was a two-bedroom, concrete block house. Joy and I, with our new-born baby, moved into the two bedrooms. We bought some wooden benches and put them in the living room. My grandfather, Arnold Shreve, built us a pulpit and that became our first church in Orange Park. We lived in the rest of the house and the living room became our church. We held our first service on July 4, 1959. To begin with, we only had our small family and my grandparents as our congregation. Finances were tight, so we paid rent to the church for the use of the parsonage. Joy enjoys telling people to this day that we paid them to let us preach in Orange Park! I've looked at some of my sermon outlines, and I think they got short-changed! I'm sure there will be a special spot in heaven for all those folks that put up with that cocky, young, 20-year old pastor in 1959 and 60.

Our stay in Orange Park only lasted about two years, during which time we built a small concrete block auditorium in which to meet. It was just in time, too! Our family was growing and we needed our living space. David and Steven came along in rapid-fire order, and then we were five! The church grew slowly but steadily. On the second anniversary of our beginning we had a record attendance of 47! That was to be the high attendance mark of our pastorate in Orange Park. In 1961, we resigned in order to go back to Southeastern to finish up my bachelor's degree and prepare for further ministry.

Today, there stands a beautiful, vibrant church on the very same piece of property that we purchased in 1959. They have since acquired adjacent property and have expanded their buildings to house a large Christian school. They have made a significant impact on their city. Numerous pastors and missionaries have come out of that church and it continues to be a spiritual force in Clay County, Florida .

MOBILE, ALABAMA

After graduating from Southeastern in 1962, our family of five moved temporarily back to Jacksonville to concentrate on looking for a church to pastor. I heard that there was a camp meeting starting in Hurley, Mississippi, a ten-hour drive from Jacksonville. I packed a few clothes, hopped into our little two-tone cream and maroon Simca sedan and headed off for parts unknown.

I haven't been back to Hurley, Mississippi in over 40 years and I don't know how it might have changed during that time. However, in 1962 the campground was in a remote wooded area, far removed from civilization. I followed the directions I had been given and finally came to the remote cluster of buildings that made up the Mississippi District Campgrounds for the Assemblies of God. I knew absolutely nobody in Mississippi; and furthermore, absolutely nobody knew me. When I drove on the campground, I saw an older gentleman in a pair of bib overalls with a hammer and nails in his hand. As he headed in my direction to check out this stranger, I assumed that he was the caretaker.

"Can I help you?" he asked, obviously wondering who I was.

"My name is Arnold Lastinger," I replied. "I've just graduated from Southeastern Bible College and I'm looking for a place to pastor. I understand that you're having a camp meeting here this week and I thought I might make some contacts or hear about some open churches." He hesitated for a moment as his eyes intently looked me over. With the wisdom that only comes from years of experience, he made a quick judgment of my character. I'm sure he sensed that I was flat broke and in desperate need. To my surprise, he introduced himself as the district superintendent of the Mississippi district.

"I need somebody to collect money in the cafeteria," he said. "If you will collect money from the people going through the line, I'll give you free room and board for the week while you're here." It was an answer to prayer and I gladly accepted. He gave me a money bag with some change in it and I checked into the dorm to get ready for the night service.

There was a large crowd attending the camp meeting and after dinner my money bag was bulging with the receipts from dinner. I locked the money in the trunk of my car and got ready for the evening service. After church I began to circulate around, introducing myself and trying to make friends with the total strangers at the meeting. I happened to overhear a group of pastors talking.

"If you know of anyone who is looking for a church, I resigned last Sunday!" one of them said. Sensing my opportunity, I tapped him on the shoulder.

"I couldn't help but overhear that you resigned last Sunday. Do you mind telling me where the church is and who I should contact?" I said.

"Not at all," W.O. Stephens replied. "It's Moffatt Road Assembly of God in Mobile, Alabama." He gave me directions to the church and the name of the man who was serving as the chairman of the board.

The next day, after lunch, I locked the moneybag in the trunk and headed off for the 45-minute drive to Mobile from Hurley. I had no idea what to expect, but the timing was just too "coincidental" for me to ignore. I drove directly to the church. It was a plain, unadorned building on the main highway going into Mobile. The little parsonage sat just west of the church building. The pastor whom I had met the night before was at home. He told me a little about the church; I was very interested. Sailors have a saying, "Any port in a storm!" At that point, I didn't have any other options and Moffatt Road looked like a pretty good port. Pastor Stephens gave me directions to the head deacon's house and I decided to pay him a visit.

I drove to his ranch-style house on a large, country lot not far from the church. Although it was the middle of the afternoon in the middle of the week, a number of cars were parked in the yard when I arrived. I knocked on the door and a man answered. Looking me over suspiciously, he asked,

"Something I can do for you?" I looked beyond him into the living room and saw a group of men sitting in a circle. Fearing that I had interrupted something important, I said,

"My name is Arnold Lastinger. I'm from Jacksonville, Florida. I've just graduated from Southeastern Bible College and I understand you are looking for a pastor." His face brightened and his suspicions fell to the floor like broken glass.

"Do come in," he said, "This is our deacon board. We are meeting to decide what direction to go in finding a pastor. We'd love to talk to you."

I went around the circle introducing myself to each of the men. The oldest in the group was quietly looking me over with a very curious eye. At last he spoke,

"Lastinger did you say? You're not Sweet Lastinger, are you?" I tried to conceal my shock at his question. My mind was racing at breakneck speed. In my father's younger years he had been nicknamed "Sweet" Lastinger. Knowing that he had quite a colorful past, I didn't quite know how to answer this question. Finally, I spoke.

"What do you know about Sweet Lastinger?" I nervously asked.

"Well, I know that his step-mother is my sister," he said. My mouth dropped open.

"You mean, you're Grandma Carrie's brother," I asked.

"Then you must be Sweet's boy!" Brother Jarvis said as he reached out to hug me. The ice was broken and we were ready to talk.

"We need a pastor who will commit to us for the long haul," one of them said to me. "Every pastor we've ever had has used us for a stepping stone to a bigger church. None of them has ever truly had our best interests at heart. We want someone who will stay with us and grow with us." I was young, naïve and inexperienced. I swallowed that line, "hook, line and sinker" as they say.

"Well, I'm your man," I said, "I want to be a part of a great work for God." I did not find out until sometime later that the church had been in existence for only six years and I was to be the seventh pastor in six years. Every pastor had left under pressure from the church board!

(PLEASE NOTE: In the interest of truth and honesty, I have tried to be as factual as I could in this account. I regret that my

report of our Moffatt Road experience will make the church appear in a very unfavorable light. Please remember, that was another time, another congregation, and another board. Over 40 years have passed since that time and I'm sure the church has changed significantly in those years. Recent reports that I have heard from Mobile paint the church in a much better light.)

"Can you preach for us this weekend?" the board asked. I assured them that I could and the meeting broke up. With rising excitement, I jumped into my little car and headed for the nearest public pay phone. I found a shopping center with a phone booth in the suburbs of Mobile. With pounding heart, I grabbed the moneybag and went into the phone booth. From the cafeteria moneybag, I carefully counted out the change that I needed for the telephone and replaced it with cash from my own wallet. I laid the moneybag on the shelf in the phone booth and nervously dialed Joy's number in Jacksonville. "Guess what, honey! I've found us a church!" I said. "I'll be home Friday to pick you up and we'll drive back to Mobile on Saturday. "I'll be ready," she said and we hung up the phone. I replaced the receiver back in the cradle and walked out of the phone booth to my car, leaving the moneybag lying on the shelf of the phone booth in a busy shopping center in Mobile.

I drove the 45-minute drive back to the campground rejoicing in what I believed to be God's provision. In retrospect, it probably was. My 30 months at Moffatt Road taught me more about pastoring than Southeastern ever could have taught me. I arrived back in Hurley just in time for the evening meal in the cafeteria. When I started looking around for the moneybag so that I could do my duties in the dinner line, I suddenly remembered exactly where I had left it. With a heart pounding with sheer terror, I delegated my duties to someone else, jumped into my car and headed back to Mobile in hopes of retrieving the moneybag. I broke every speed law in the book. Crying and praying, I envisioned my ministry crashing and burning before it ever even got off the launch pad. Who would believe that I had lost the money? They knew absolutely nothing about me. I was a total stranger to all of them. As fast as I could, I drove straight to the shopping center, jumped out of my car, ran into the phone booth and picked up the moneybag, exactly where I had left it three hours earlier! No doubt, hundreds of people had passed by that phone booth, but not one of them either saw the moneybag or picked it up. God had saved my ministry! Not the first time—and certainly not the last!

The weekend at Moffat Road seemed to be a perfect match and by Sunday night we had been elected pastor by an overwhelming vote! At last, we were on our way—but to where? Time would tell. After the election, the youngest member of the deacon board came to us and gave us his credit card. "Put all your gasoline on my card," he said, "I'm taking care of your moving expense!" Grateful and awed by his generosity, I accepted the card. How could he know that I didn't have money to move? And how could I know that his motives weren't all that pure? We drove the long trip back to Jacksonville, loaded all our belongings onto a 4' by 8' utility trailer and moved our growing family to Mobile. We were now the pastors of our second church.

Our 2 ½ years at Moffatt Road should have been happy years. They certainly started out that way. We seemed to be well received by the people and the church began to grow. There was one ominous event, however, which was a harbinger of things to come. The same young couple who had given us their credit card to pay our gasoline for the move to Mobile invited us to go bowling with them one Saturday night. Joy and I both loved to bowl and we wanted to build some good social relationships in the church, so we gladly accepted. We had an enjoyable evening and we went to bed that night secure that we had done a good thing.

The next morning when we arrived at Sunday School there seemed to be a dark cloud hanging over the church. I wasn't sure what was wrong but it sure felt like something was. I didn't have to wait long for an answer. One of the deacons came to me and said,

"Sister Shirley Mae (not her real name) is not here this morning; she's at home sick." Shirley Mae was the wife of another deacon and I surely didn't want to miss this opportunity to minister to her in her time of need.

"Nothing serious," I said questioningly, "how can I help?"

"Oh, she's not physically sick," he said, "she's heartsick!"

"What can I do?" I asked.

"Well, you might want to go see her," he said, "she's heartsick about you. She heard that her pastor was seen at a local bowling alley last night, and she can't believe you would frequent such a place!"

As soon as church was over I went straight to Shirley Mae's house to try to mend some fences. "I understand that something I have done has offended you," I said, "What can I do to make it right?" The story she told me was almost incredible. It seems that my newfound "friends," the same ones who had given me their credit card and invited us for a night of bowling had intentionally created a crisis for me. They knew that Shirley Mae had a strong conviction against bowling; it had created a problem between her and a former pastor as well. As soon as they got home from bowling with us they had called her and said,

"You'll never guess who we saw at the bowling alley tonight—none other than our very own pastor!" As humbly as I could, I apologized to Shirley Mae.

"If my bowling offends you, Sister," I said, "I will not bowl as long as I am your pastor." She was satisfied and I went home a little wiser than I had come. I knew now that I had a trouble maker in the church. What I was too naïve to realize at the time was that Shirley Mae, herself was a controller and a manipulator who used her influence and position in the church to get her way.

Amazingly, despite the unrest on the church board, the church began to grow. The excitement in the services attracted people and we began to attract new families. As a result our attendance figures began to climb and the offerings increased. I couldn't understand, however, why we didn't seem to be able to hang on to the new people. As quickly as they came they would leave again and go to other churches. In desperation, I approached some of those who had left us for other churches, asking the reason for their departures. "It's not you, Pastor," they said, "it's just that we were made to feel very unwelcome in the church. The people who have been there for years wouldn't even shake our hands; they would turn and walk away when we would try to start a conversation. We didn't want to have to push ourselves on them; it's easier to go somewhere else." Sadly, I left those people to go to their new churches. I had discovered one more in a large list of problems that existed in my church.

One night I received a phone call from my "friend" who had loaned me his credit card. "Dad and I would like to come over for a few minutes if you have time," he said. His wife's elderly father also served on the church board. He was a good man who had been very good to us over the months that we had been his pastors. However, he was very easily led and he really doted on his daughter, the baby in the family. The phone call had an ominous sound to it and I didn't know what to expect when they arrived. I invited them into the living room and they sat down. He wasted no time getting down to the point of his visit.

"We are here to ask for your resignation," he said abruptly.

"But, I don't feel that God is through with us here," I said, "He has not released us, yet!"

"Well, I'll be blunt," he said, "If you don't resign we are going to circulate a petition asking for your resignation."

"I'll pray about this from now to Sunday," I said. "If God releases me to resign, I'll resign on Sunday morning. If I don't resign, go ahead and get your petition." They left and I spent a restless night trying to sleep.

The next day just happened to be Sectional Council in Mobile and I requested a meeting with the sectional committee and the district officials. A very nervous 24-year old young pastor walked into that roomful of august, experienced pastors and leaders in our denomination.

"A couple of my deacons have asked for my resignation and have threatened to petition me out," I said, "but, I have not felt a release from God to go."

I laid out my case before the committee and they listened attentively. Fortunately, one of them had once pastored the same church and he knew the people I was naming very well. When I finished, the superintendent, T. H. Spence, asked me to wait outside the committee room while they discussed their recommendations to me. In a few minutes he came out to see me.

"This church has always been a troubled church," he said. "If you do what is best for you and your family, you will go home, pack your bags, brush the dust off your feet, and leave without saying 'goodbye.' But, if you do what is best for the church, you will stay and make them do what they are threatening to do. If you choose to do that, I promise you that I will make them do it 'by the book.'"

Encouraged by the committee's support, I went home with a determination to stay the course and see what happened. In my youthful idealism, it seemed like the noble thing to do at the time. If I had known then what I know today, I'm not sure I would have put my family through what we went through in the months ahead. The trouble-making deacon could not get the rest of the board to join with him in calling for my resignation. Furthermore, he was unable to get enough signatures on his petition to call for a business meeting to vote for my removal from office. Instead, they started withholding their tithes and convincing others to do the same in order to starve us out. I ultimately ended up having to get a job as auditor at a local motel in order to provide for my family. My antagonists would come to Sunday School; stay through the morning service until it came time for me to preach, and then make a big show of getting up and walking out before I could preach. It was heartbreaking to see adults acting so childishly. They finally gave up hope of running us off and left to go to another church.

They had done their damage, however. They and their parents had been charter members of the church. Even though the people in the church did not approve of the tactics they had used in an effort to get rid of us, they still blamed us for breaking up the church family. Our days were numbered at Moffatt Road. It was just a matter of time.

A few months later was the time for our annual business meeting at which time we were scheduled for a vote of confidence that would decide whether we would remain as their pastor. In those days, pastors were voted upon at every annual business meeting. I had no delusions; I knew how the vote was going to go. I even knew exactly who was going to vote for me and who was going to vote against me. I desperately prayed for God to release me and allow me to resign with dignity instead of being voted out in shame. But, I kept hearing God's "No!" I went into the business meeting knowing what the outcome would be; but, I was at peace. I knew I was not disobeying God. Not surprisingly, the business meeting went exactly as I expected; I suffered the shame of being voted out.

God had proven Himself faithful however. During the long battle for survival at the church, I began to question the call of God in my life. I wondered if God had even called me into ministry. If I was in His will, how could things be going so wrong? Two things happened, however, that served as anchors for us during that stormy time.

Joy and I left our boys with a baby-sitter and went to a Minister's Retreat at Oak Mountain State Park in north Alabama. We desperately needed refreshing and we were hungry for God to do something in our lives. One night during the service, there came a message in tongues followed by an interpretation that was like a spiritual transfusion to our spirits. I vividly remember the words of that message. "I know the battle that you are engaged in," God said, "But the battle is not yours, it is mine. Do not fight the battle; I will fight for you. Just stand still and see the salvation of the Lord. And, know this; The Lord will vindicate that which is right!" I knew I was right! After all, I was standing on biblical principles. We went home from Oak Mountain with a new determination to stay the course.

On another occasion during that difficult time I was invited to preach in a church on the east side of Mobile bay. In addition to my pastoral responsibilities, I was working full time at the Albert Pick motel in Mobile. I did not have much time to prepare a sermon for that night. After I got off from work I was driving across the Mobile causeway with my Bible open in the seat beside me, desperately praying for God to give me something worthwhile to say when I arrived at the church. My eyes fell on Isaiah 6, "In the year that King Uzziah died I saw the Lord..." The text seemed to supernaturally come alive as I was reading it. A logical, three-point outline fell into place. By the time I got to the church the anointing of God was all over me and I could hardly wait to get to the pulpit.

Much to my surprise, the little church was packed with people. There was not a single unoccupied seat in the entire building! And, there were almost as many standing outside the little country church looking in through the open windows. When the pastor introduced me to preach I began to give them what God had given to me just minutes earlier. The Holy Spirit came down in that service in a way that I had never seen prior to that time. It was akin to what God did in Brownsville 30 years later in the Pensacola Outpouring. The altar filled with people weeping and crying out to God. I had to walk on the top of the altar railing in order to get to where people were standing. Every person that I touched fell to the floor, slain by the power of God. I had never had anything like that happen to me before! It was breath-taking. To this day, I don't have words to describe what happened that night. On the way home in the quietness of my car I was still basking in the light of God's anointing when the Holy Spirit whispered to my spirit, "You see, Son, I did call you to preach!" From that point on, I had no more doubts.

After the business meeting we served out our thirty days at Moffatt Road as required by the bylaws. During that time we candidated for the First Assembly of God in Slocomb, Alabama and were elected by a unanimous vote. We went directly from Mobile to Slocomb. One chapter of our lives was closed and another one had begun.

"First Assembly of God, Slocomb, Alabama; 1964"

SLOCOMB, ALABAMA

First Assembly in Slocomb was everything we needed. Moffatt Road had left us beaten down and discouraged; Slocomb took us in and wrapped us up with love. We fell deeply in love with these people and we healed quickly. Slocomb was a tiny country town with one traffic light, a bank, a post office, two grocery stores and little else. The 1200 people all seemed to know each other and it was a tightly-knit community. Even so, they took our family of outsiders in and welcomed us as their own.

We were young and we began to attract young people. Teenagers were drawn to us and we were able to minister to them. One young girl gave her heart to the Lord and made a dramatic turnaround from a wild life of sin. She was so turned on for Jesus that she asked our youth leader if she could give her testimony the following week. There was a record-breaking crowd there that night. When she shared what God had done in her life, she took the liberty of asking how many others there would like for Jesus to do the same thing for them. To my amazement, 32 teenagers responded. The altars were filled with young people weeping and crying out to God for forgiveness. Joy and I, with our youth leader were the only adults present to pray for them. I ran back to the telephone and began calling parents. "Revival has broken out in the youth group," I said, "I need you here to help us pray for them!" Although some of those young people have fallen by the wayside, many of them are still actively involved in the work of the Kingdom to this very day.

Slocomb played a very significant role in our lives in that it became a place of healing and encouragement to us. But, our stay there was to be short-lived. We were young and ambitious and small-town Slocomb did not provide us with much of a challenge or an opportunity to build a great work for God. At the end of three years, in the spring of 1967 we resigned our pastorate and bid a tearful farewell to our beloved congregation at the First Assembly of God in Slocomb. To this day, my heart swells with fondness when I remember those days in Slocomb.

"Our Family in Thomasville, Georgia; 1967"

"First Assembly Choir, Thomasville, Georgia; 1970"

THOMASVILLE, GEORGIA

Thomasville, Georgia is a beautiful city whose streets are landscaped with azaleas, covered with a canopy of dogwood trees and lined by beautiful antebellum homes. It is justifiably called "The City of 10,000 Roses." 20,000 happy people lived there and we made it 20,006! At that time, First Assembly was a boxy-looking brick church located on Wolcott Street in a declining section of town. But, we didn't care. The people loved us and we felt warmly welcomed.

As in Slocomb, our ministry seemed to be especially targeted at the youth. Our youth group grew and revival broke out among our young people. Today, there are many who have become ministers of the gospel. I can think of at least seven who became involved in pastoral ministry, and one who became a Bible College professor.

We started a choir in Thomasville and they became quite good. In fact, we courageously boarded an old school bus with no air-conditioning and took a week-long tour of Alabama, Tennessee and Georgia singing in different churches every night. Come to think of it, we probably weren't that good! But, what we lacked in talent, we made up for with enthusiasm. They were happy days and we loved every minute of it.

We spent five happy years in Thomasville and they were years of growth, both for us and for the church. We had all the normal church problems that one always has when you put a group of people together. But, there was nothing that God did not equip us to handle. We were content and happy that God had called us there.

AMERICUS, GEORGIA

One day a call came from our District Superintendent, Brother Aaron Wall. "Brother Lastinger," he said, "I have a church in Americus, Georgia that has asked us to find them a pastor and I think you just might be the man for them."

"I'm honored that you would ask," I said, "but, what makes you think I would fit there?"

"Well," he said, "they're a good church that's had some problems. They've just voted a pastor out and the church is evenly divided over whether he should go or stay. They don't want to split and they have requested the district to step in and assume the government of the church for one year and to find them a pastor. We think you might be the man!"

"Our Family in Americus, Georgia; 1973"

    I really was not looking to leave Thomasville. There had been moments when I thought I would like a new challenge somewhere else, but the thought had passed and we had settled in, secure in our pastorate in Thomasville. However, I wanted to keep my heart open to God and I was reluctant to slam the door on what may be God's invitation to a new chapter in our lives. I told Bro. Wall that I would go preach for them for one weekend, look the situation over and make a decision based on what I found there. My plan was to preach for them and then take a confidential straw vote of the people to let me know how the people felt about my coming. Although I told no one about my criterion, I wanted a 100% vote of the congregation if I was to consider going to Americus. When I counted the votes, I must say that I was somewhat relieved that I had slightly less than a unanimous vote. At least the matter was settled; I would be staying in Thomasville. The matter was not to be settled by a congregational vote, however; their pastor was to be appointed by the district. So, the people left the meeting that night, not knowing if they had a pastor or not.

On the following Thursday the sectional council convened in our church and I was to meet with Bro. Wall in his hotel room in Thomasville. As I settled into my chair in his room the inevitable question came.

"Well, have you made a decision about Americus?" he said. Not surprised by the abruptness of his question, I thought I was ready with an answer.

"Yes, I have," I said, "I'm not going, I'm staying where I am." If you have not experienced it yourself it is difficult to explain what happened next. As soon as the words were out of my mouth, I felt this gnawing anxiety in the pit of my stomach and an overwhelming sense that I had made the wrong choice. No handwriting on the wall, no booming voice, no Damascus Road experience, just a gnawing feeling of discomfort. I knew in that instant that I would be the next pastor in Americus, Georgia. My dilemma now was how to gracefully change my mind. I didn't want my superintendent to think I was fickle and indecisive. I didn't want to say, "No, wait! That's wrong. I want to change my mind!" Instead, I began to ask him more questions about the church and board in Americus. I'm sure that in his years of collected wisdom he knew that my decision was far from final. He listened to me politely and answered all my questions. Finally, however, he looked intently into my eyes and said,

"You still haven't made up your mind, have you?"

"Yes, I have," I said, "I'm going to Americus!" He grinned and said,

"I thought so." The feeling in the pit of my stomach changed from discomfort to intense peace; I knew I had found the will of God.

Roughly the same population as Thomasville, Americus presented a different set of challenges, however. The culture was more agrarian, dependent on peanuts and cotton. Early in our ministry there, I was invited to preach in Montgomery, Alabama. I was driving home late at night and was growing sleepy as I drove along. I decided to pray, in hopes of waking myself up and, at the same time get to spend some time with our Father.

"Father, I don't know how to pastor in Americus," I said, "I need your help. Would you please give me a key to reaching this community with the gospel?" As I was driving along north of Auburn, Alabama headed toward home, I heard an inaudible but forceful voice from God saying,

"What about radio?" A little surprised by the force with which The Voice spoke, I responded,

"But, I don't know anything about radio, Father!"

"But, I do!" He said, with a pronounced emphasis on the pronoun, "I." "I will teach you." For the next hour, ideas flooded into my mind. I would approach the local radio station about buying some time. I would then sell that time to sponsors and I would play Southern Gospel music for that hour each day. I would use that time to be a witness for Jesus and to get my name and our church's name before the public eye.

By the time I got home in the wee hours of the morning, I was so charged up that I could hardly sleep. When the daylight dawned, I jumped out of bed and called one of my deacons, Carlos Bailey, comptroller for a local manufacturing company.

"Can we go to breakfast, Carlos?" I asked, "I've got something to run by you." We arranged to meet and I shared what had happened to me during my late night drive from Montgomery. Carlos got almost as excited as I was.

"The owner of the station is a friend of mine!" he said. "Let's go see him!" In a matter of minutes we were in Carlos' car headed for his friend's house.

We drove up to the station owner's beautiful home to find him chopping firewood for his fireplace. He took off his gloves, wiped the sweat from his brow and shook my hand. "Pleased to meet you, Preacher," he said, "Any friend of Carlos is a friend of mine!" I shared my idea with him and watched as his expression softened and then turned into excitement. He heard me out and then said, "Preacher, my station is a rock station. But, I have some requests for some Christian music. I've been wanting to block in some Christian music, but I don't have anybody on my staff that knows anything about gospel music. I like your idea; I believe it's doable!" Before we left we had negotiated a price for one hour per day, five days a week at 10:00 each morning—the perfect time! The date was set and "The Americus Gospel Music Hour" was born!

I took to Southern Gospel music like a duck takes to water. It was a perfect fit. I purposely kept my program unprofessional. I wanted it to be a folksy, down-home, program that people would love to listen to and interact with. We took call-in requests. I only took sponsors that I approved of and whose products I actually used or endorsed. The commercials were off-the-cuff and highly personalized. I never lacked for sponsors; they lined up waiting for an opportunity to be on the broadcast. When our one-year contract expired, the station owner came to me to ask if I would consider expanding to two hours, from 10:00-12:00 each weekday. It seemed like a good idea, so we agreed and "The Americus Gospel Music Hour" became "The Americus Gospel Music Time."

The program became the most widely listened-to program in the area. My name and the church's name were recognized by almost everybody in the listening area. It opened many doors for me to present the gospel in many different venues. I had asked God for a key to reach my community with the gospel. The key He gave me was gospel music; and, the key worked. First Assembly in Americus was on the map; it became a viable influence for Christ in Sumter County. The church tripled in attendance and many people came to know Jesus.

Our roots sank deep into the South Georgia clay. We bought a home and our boys grew into young men. Three of them graduated from high school and enrolled in the local college. Seven years passed and it seemed as if we had found a permanent home at last. But, God had another idea! That, however, is the subject for the next chapter in our lives.

Chapter Four

Gainesville:
We Almost Didn't Come!

It was a little after 11:00 on a Saturday night in the spring of 1979 and Joy and I had just settled down for a good night's sleep, anticipating a good day of services the next day. I was just about to turn out the table lamp when the bedside phone rang.

"Is this Arnold Lastinger?" asked the voice on the other end of the line.

"Yes, it is," I answered, "May I help you?"

"I'll bet you'll never guess who this is," the voice said. That's not a game I like to play and I tried to conceal the annoyance in my voice when I responded,

"No, I don't believe I can."

"This is Bud Taylor," he said. Bud and I had been young people in the church together when I was a brand new Christian in the mid-1950's. He was a little older than I was and he also served as my Sunday School teacher for a while. However, Bud moved away to Bartow, Florida and I went away to Bible College and we had not had any contact for over 18 years. Now, I was hearing his pleasant southern drawl after all those years. "We're looking for a pastor and our board would like to know if you are interested in being considered as a candidate," he asked.

"Thanks, Bud, but no; we are quite happy where we are," I answered.

Joy and I were about to celebrate seven years as pastors of the First Assembly of God in Americus, Georgia. They had been good years and the church had grown significantly during that time. We had a good ministry there and, because of our radio ministry, we had made quite an impact upon the entire area. This was during the years of the Jimmy Carter presidency, and Americus was the "big city" where the Carter family came to buy groceries and do their shopping. Everybody in the county knew who we were and where we pastored. I served on several community committees and was on a first-name basis with the mayor and sheriff. We were enjoying being "big fish in a little pond."

However, there had been one big cloud on the horizon of happiness I have just described. We had a dear sister named Jean (not her real name) in the church who was suffering through an agonizing and emotionally disturbing menopause. She was normally a sweet and charming woman with the very best of social graces and a deep love for Jesus. On top of all that, she was probably the most influential person in the whole church. She was the church organist and taught an adult Sunday School class. And, she was a professor at the local college with equal influence and impact there. However, about once a month she turned into a different person, deeply paranoid and totally convinced that everybody in the church was out to get her.

Joy was too young to have experienced that upsetting period in a woman's life and I had very little experience in dealing with this kind of problem. I spent hours in pastoral counseling with her, not realizing that counseling is totally ineffective in dealing with scrambled hormones. I would give her what I thought was sage advice. However, when she quoted it back to me, she had heard something totally different from what I had said. I was at wit's end and ready to throw up my hands and quit. I even considered finding another pastorate where I wouldn't have to deal with that problem—whatever "that problem" was!

We had visited the First Assembly of God in Niagara Falls, New York on vacation a year earlier. They had put us on their mailing list and we were receiving their weekly bulletins. I noticed that their pastor had resigned and that they were beginning a pastoral search. This seemed to be the opportunity we were looking for. I sent them a résumé and eagerly awaited their response. In a few days, I received a phone call asking if we could fly up to candidate for them on a weekend. We made arrangements to do so and a few days later we checked into the Holiday Inn in Niagara Falls. It was love at first sight! I had reservations about how this guy from the Deep South would fit with these "New York Yankees" but it was as though we had been friends for many years. We met for the interview with the board on Saturday. They asked all the right questions and we gave all the right answers. On Sunday morning, the glory of God came down and we had a wonderful altar service. On Sunday evening we had a "fireside chat" with the congregation and gave them an opportunity to ask anything they wanted to ask. Then, we had a reception afterward, and I was already beginning to feel like their pastor. Their business session was not to be held until Monday night, so we flew home on Monday morning. I was so confident that this was the will of God for us that we began to make notes on what we needed to do to make the move to snow country, USA! When the phone rang late Monday night, I answered, fully confident that we were going to be told that we had been elected by a unanimous vote. Imagine my shock and disappointment when the chairman told me that we had missed being elected by just one vote!

I think my biggest disappointment was that I could have missed the will of God so easily. I was so convinced that this was God's will for our lives! I have since come to realize that once you become emotionally involved in a decision your objectivity goes out the window. I wanted to be away from Americus and the menopausal problem so badly that I was ready to hop on the first boat leaving town! But, that was not God's plan. He did not want me to run away from the problem; He wanted me to learn how to deal with it.

Not just a little bit angry with God, I decided to pout about it. "OK, God. If you want me to stay in Americus, Georgia the rest of my life, I'm up to the challenge. I'll never send out another résumé or make another phone call. If you ever want me to leave here, you're gonna have to meet three criteria. (1) They're going to have to call me; I won't initiate the contact. (2) It will have to be a growing church. I don't want to have to build any fires with wet wood. And, (3) it will have to be a city of at least 100,000 people. If I'm going to move, I want a shot at a lot of people. I don't want to move from Smallville, USA to Tinytown, America. Convinced that God could not meet all three of those criteria, I settled in for the long haul in Americus, Ga.

One Sunday morning after the Niagara trip, Jean met me at the back door of the church.

"Pastor, we need to talk!" she said.

"Oh no," I groaned to myself. "Not another fruitless counseling session." Reluctantly, I followed her back to my office. Three hours later, we were no closer to a solution than we had ever been. In exasperation, I finally said to her, "Woman, go see your doctor; you're a sick woman!" I didn't know whether she would slap me or stalk out of my office. To my surprise, she wilted and slouched down in a chair behind her.

"You could be right," she said, "My husband has been telling me that for months." Relieved, I begged her to make an appointment with her gynecologist the very next day. She called me after her doctor's appointment to tell me that the doctor had put her on Hormone Replacement Therapy.

"Never in my entire career, have I met a woman whose hormones were so out of balance," he had told her. "You must be a terror to live with!"

"That's what my husband and my pastor have told me," she responded. Within a week of beginning HRT she was the same, sweet, southern lady that I had known for seven years. If only we had known a few months earlier; I wish all counseling problems were so easily solved! I did not know it then, but I had learned the lesson God wanted me to learn. My time in Americus was about to come to an end.

COMING TO CANDIDATE

Bud sounded disappointed with my negative response to his question. I had hardly gotten the words out of my mouth when I remembered the three criteria that I had given to God after the Niagara weekend. It suddenly dawned on me that I had not initiated this contact; they had called me. Although I had already declined his invitation, I asked Bud to tell me a little about the church.

"We're bursting at the seams!" he said, "We've already had to go to two services on Sunday morning. In fact, one of the first things you would have to do is to lead us in a building program if you came to be our pastor." A growing church! I was revisiting my second criteria that I had given God a few months earlier. I swallowed hard and asked Bud one more question.

"Tell me Bud, what is the population of Gainesville?" Chill bumps came up on my arms as I heard his answer,

"About 100,000, give or take a few!" he said. In a two-minute phone conversation, God had met the three criteria that I was sure He would never meet. What an awesome God!

I let my negative answer to Bud stand. I needed time to process this. I asked Joy if she was interested in making the move to Gainesville and she gave me a flat "No!" Boys in college, a new home of our own, too many roots to pull up. Her nesting instincts were working overtime. She wasn't interested.

I tried to sleep, but tossed and turned all night long. Before dawn, I got up, dressed, went to the church and hastily typed up a résumé to send to Gainesville. True to my promise to God, I did not have one already prepared. Before Sunday School I went to the Post Office and dropped the document in the mail. I called Bud and told him what I had done.

"Let's just see where the Lord leads in this matter, Bud," I said.

"We'll go over your résumé on Tuesday night," he said, and we hung up the phone.

My phone rang late Tuesday night. "Can you preach for us this coming Sunday?" Bud asked.

"As a matter of fact, I already have a guest speaker filling my pulpit," I responded. "We'll be there!" What I did not know for years to come was that God had already confirmed to the board in that Tuesday night meeting that I was to be their pastor. Joy and I met with the board and their wives the following Saturday for dinner. It was a congenial meeting and we had a great time. Sunday morning went wonderfully well, and again, we had a "fireside chat" meeting with the congregation on Sunday night. They asked some very provocative questions, but the meeting went well. Joy and I retired to the pastor's office to await the congregation's vote.

Earlier in the day, at the hotel, I had already begun to feel that this was God's plan for us. However, I was still smarting from the Niagara incident and I didn't want to miss God again. Hoping that God would confirm His will through two different minds, I asked Joy if she felt that it was God's will for us to come to Gainesville.

She told me that she had not changed her mind; she didn't want to leave Americus. Dejected and disappointed with her answer, I awaited service time that night. Now, sitting in the pastor's office, it was decision time.

"Honey, I know in my spirit that when the board chairman comes walking through that door he is going to ask us to be their pastor. We need to have an answer. Do you still feel the same?"

"When you asked me that question this afternoon, I told you 'No'," my wife said. "But, I immediately felt checked in my spirit, as if I had said the wrong thing. If they offer us the position, I think we should take that as God's will and accept it." At that point, I knew we would be moving to Gainesville.

In a few minutes Buddy Morrison came walking into the room. In his characteristically humorous way, Buddy said,

"I have good news and bad news. The good news is that we want you to be our pastor; the bad news is that you have 4 votes against you. If you need more time to make a decision, by all means take it; we can wait."

"No, Buddy," I said, "You folks have prayed and we have prayed, and I think we have all heard from God. We will accept your call." Never the shy one, Buddy threw his arms around me and began to cry,

"Praise God! Praise God! Praise God!" he wept. He escorted us out to the auditorium and up to the platform. "Ladies and gentlemen," he said very theatrically, "It gives me great pleasure to introduce our new pastors!" I was not prepared for what happened next; sheer pandemonium broke loose. The people clapped; they cheered, they whistled, they stomped their feet, and they shouted praises to God. I knew we had come home!

That March night in 1979 changed our lives forever. In the very first month that we were there, I felt the Holy Spirit assuring me that He had been grooming me all my life for our ministry in Gainesville. I felt that I would spend the rest of my life in Gainesville. There would be no other church for me. I shared with the congregation that I was committing the rest of my life to this church; that I was there for the long haul. In return, I began to feel their commitment to me as their pastor. It was the beginning of a long and happy relationship.

SETTLING IN FOR THE LONG HAUL

What began that night was a 25-year honeymoon in which I was the groom and my congregation was the bride. In 25 years, I never considered leaving and I never sent out a single résumé to another church. I meant what I said—I was there to stay. Not that there were no problems. I immediately sensed that I was a duck out of water. I had grown accustomed to being the big fish in a little pond, in a city where everybody knew my name. Now, I was a nobody in a large city where nobody even knew who I was—nor did they care! I had traded a small-town agricultural, Bible-belt culture for a big city university culture with few moral restraints. Talk about a culture shock! The first month we were there, a bank patron was blown away by a shotgun blast at the night depository just a few blocks from our house! And, a homosexual college professor was murdered in a satanic ritualistic slaying in a motel room near the campus. This was our initiation as pastors in big-city Gainesville, Florida!

I knew that God had sent me to Gainesville, but I knew right away that I did not have what it took to pastor in this city. Everything I had learned about pastoring in Americus, Georgia would not work in Gainesville, Florida. I went desperately to my knees and prayed that prayer that every pastor knows so well, "Hellllllllllllllllp! Please God," I prayed, "Show me the key to pastoring in Gainesville, Florida." It seemed as though I heard one word in my spirit. Relationships! Just one word; but, I knew exactly what God was telling me. Begin by building relationships.

I began with those closest to me. I started calling my board members and inviting them to lunch with me. We would invite a board member and his wife to go out to dinner on Friday nights. We purposely drove to Cedar Key, an hour's drive away, so that we would have more time together to get to know each other better. We would have cookouts at our house and invite the board over for the evening. Discussing church business was taboo; this was to be a time of relationship building. And, it worked! We began to fall in love with each other. I grew to trust these men and their wives; and, they trusted me.

At the end of the year, I told the men what God had told me about relationships. "That's what I've done with you this year," I told them, "Now; I want you to do the same thing with the other families in the church. Pick out a circle of friends and build relationships with them so that they become dear friends and not just acquaintances from church." They took me at my word and began to build their network of friends. Out of that humble beginning was birthed the cell group ministry that still is the lifeblood of that church to this very day.

I FOUND A CHOIR DIRECTOR!

Shortly after our arrival at the church, the board sponsored a reception for us in the fellowship hall. Somehow, I ended up seated across the table from a young man named Joe Jamerson. Someone had told me that Joe had been a music major and had once taught band in a public school. Although he was now a debit-collecting insurance agent, I knew he had not forgotten all he had learned about music.

"Joe," I confidently said, "I want you to be my choir director!" Joe scoffed and said,

"No, I don't think you really want that! Vocal music is not my cup of tea; I'm more of an instrumentalist." It took a little persuasion, but by the time I left the reception that night, I had a new choir director.

I had mistakenly assumed that Joe was a born-again Christian. After all, he looked the part! He had been raised in an Assembly of God family. He cut his teeth on AG pews, sat in AG Sunday School classes, and slouched in the pew with the rest of the teenagers in his home church in Joliet, Illinois. How could this fine, upstanding AG boy not be a Christian? But, I was destined to find out the hard way. What I did not know at the time was that Joe was leading a double life. During the week he was a hard-driving, dog-eat-dog salesman, cheating, drinking, and doing whatever it took to make a sale and to reach his goals. On Sunday, he put on his "Religious Robe" and directed the choir at the First Assembly of God. Ironically, despite

Joe's hypocrisy, the music ministry grew and reached possibly the highest heights it has ever reached in the history of our church.

Our personal relationship was tenuous at best during this time. In my 45 years of pastoring, I have never fought so hard, argued so vehemently, or dealt with such a pig-headed person as Joe Jamerson. Because I was a pastor, I probably would never have invited him outside for a brawl, but if he had invited me I would have accepted his invitation. If I had killed him, I think I could have convinced God that it was justifiable homicide!

But, God was working in Joe's life in ways that I did not know about. His marriage had begun to crumble and he was about to lose his wife and daughter. In fact, she had already left him and gone back to the Chicago area to take a job. Joe's story was that he was going to join her later, but I think he suspected that his marriage was coming to an end. Joe's life was about to change significantly, and he didn't have a clue as to what lay ahead for him.

Never thinking that Joe was God's target, one Sunday night I felt strongly impressed that this was someone's last call to the cross. I shared with the congregation what I was feeling and waited for someone to respond. Joe was standing with his trumpet on the platform behind me, curious as to whom God might be targeting. He watched, secretly relieved, as a woman came forward for prayer.

"Thank you sister, but you're not the one God is calling," he heard me say. Joe was thinking to himself, "Whoever this guy is, he must be some terrible character!" as he watched to see who would come forward. Suddenly, in his spirit, Joe heard God say,

"Joe, it's you!" Joe began to nervously bargain with God.

"OK, God, I'll make this right. I'll do business with you, but not here, and not now! Wait until I get home tonight and I'll do whatever you want me to do. Many of these people are my customers and I don't want them to know all the things I've done. They'll lose confidence in me and I'll lose customers. Not now, Lord!"

"It's now or never," he heard God say. Tearfully, Joe made his way to the altar and wept his way through to genuine repentance. All the things he didn't want anyone to know that he had done, he now heard himself confessing out loud to God for all the world to hear. At last, Mom and Dad Jamerson's prayers were answered, Joe

Jamerson—the prodigal son had come home! And, God began to put his life back together again.

Today, if I had to list my best friends in all the earth, Joe Jamerson would be near the top of the list. The man who had been my fiercest opponent had become one of my dearest friends. To quote the Christian comedian, Jerry Clower, "Ain't God good?"

My marriage to the First Assembly of God lasted for exactly 25 years and ended with a month-long celebration in April of 2004, when I turned the reins of leadership over to my young protégé, Michael Patz. Without exception, I count those years to be the happiest years of our lives.

Chapter Five
Cancer Evangelism

"Our Growing Family Gainesville, Florida; 1993"

There were seven of us children from three different fathers, but all having the same mother. None of us ever felt that we were very high on our parents' priority list. It always seemed as if they were more interested in drinking than they were in us. I was the oldest child, followed by two sisters fathered by Lewis Lastinger. He and our mother were divorced before I ever started to school. Not too long afterward, he met and married Billie Gunter, a waitress in a restaurant near where he worked in Jacksonville, Florida. As with our mother, both of them were heavy drinkers and spent most of their evenings in one of those local taverns "where everybody knows your name."

Dad and Billie were never able to have children and this seemed to be of great concern to her. Although she was never unkind to us children, it was evident to us that she resented any affection our father ever showed to us. She always seemed to hold us at arm's length and to view us as competitors for our father's attention. At one point I even heard her say to a friend, "If I had it to do over again I would never marry a man with a ready-made family!" We three children just took it in stride and chalked it up as Billie's problem—not ours. Our father, however, in order to keep peace in the family, limited any displays of affection to us in any way. We grew up thinking that's just the way it was and there wasn't much we could do about it.

The three of us grew up, got married and had our own families. I can't speak for my sisters, but I began to resent that my children were deprived of their paternal grandparents. On more than one occasion when we were visiting in Jacksonville, I would call to find out if Dad and Billie were going to be home so we could bring the children by to see them. Dad would reassure me that they would be there. But, when we got to their home they would be somewhere in their neighborhood tavern drinking beer and carousing with their barroom buddies. It took me some years and a lot of the Holy Spirit's help to work through my anger toward them for this slighting of their grandchildren.

Shortly after we came to pastor in Gainesville, Florida I received a call from Billie.

"Arnold," she said, "The doctors have diagnosed me with terminal lung cancer and I don't have long to live."

"I'm sorry to hear that, Billie," I said.

"I've been doing a lot of thinking," she said, "about you and about Jesus. I'd like to talk to you!"

"I'll be there the first thing tomorrow morning!" I said, trying to conceal the anticipation I felt in my heart. I had prayed for Dad and Billie for 27 years; at last it seemed as though I was going to see those prayers answered.

The next morning I eagerly got dressed and drove the two hours to my father's house in Jacksonville. When I arrived I found Dad and Billie sitting in the living room awaiting my arrival. In all my years of ministry, I have never seen anyone as ready to be saved as Billie was. She was like a ripe plum just barely hanging on the tree, ready to fall at the slightest touch. I explained God's unconditional love to her and how much He wanted to forgive her and adopt her into his family if only she would accept His love and forgiveness. Like the dying woman she was, she desperately reached out and embraced the gift of salvation that I offered to her. After I led her in the sinner's prayer of repentance and acceptance, she opened her eyes and looked into mine. A miraculous light had come on in her eyes, like the light of wonder and awe that a child has upon making a newfound discovery. The joy that was bubbling up inside her spilled out as she looked at me and said,

"This is the most wonderful thing that has ever happened to me; I am so happy!" Without a moment's hesitation, she looked across the room to where my Dad was sitting. "Lewis, you ought to do this," she said, "this is the most wonderful thing that has ever happened to me. I want you to have it, too!" My father squirmed in his seat, very uncomfortable in the spotlight which she had shined upon him.

"Don't worry about me, Billie," he said, "I'll be alright; you just take care of your own needs."

"But, you don't understand, Lewis; this is wonderful!" she said.

"I'll be alright," he said, "don't worry about me!"

"Dad," I said, "you really don't have a clue what she's talking about! Listen to what your wife is telling you. She's telling you that this is the best experience she has ever had in her lifetime! That's worth taking note of. Listen to her!"

I'm sure I didn't do a very good job of concealing my frustration. I had prayed for my father for so many years and he was so close; I couldn't stand to see him backing away. Yet, I knew very well the Lastinger stubbornness that I had inherited from him. I knew I could not push him or it would only drive him further away. So, I compromised with him.

"OK, Dad, I'll leave you alone to think about what has happened if you will promise me one thing; when the time comes, I want to be there. Will you call me and let me pray with you?"

"Yeah, yeah Son, no problem," he said. And the matter was closed; for the time being!

Billie had left the room and I began to look around to see where she had gone. I heard a voice in the back room and I got up to go see what was happening. I found her sitting on the bed in her room with the telephone directory open. She was calling everyone she knew to tell them what had happened to her! She was making no effort to conceal the joy and enthusiasm she felt over her newfound relationship with Jesus Christ! Wouldn't it be wonderful if we Christians never lost that evangelistic first love?

After she had finished calling everyone she could think of, she came back into the living room and sat down. About that time, a next-door beer-drinking friend came over to visit Billie. When she walked through the front door, even before she could be seated, Billie was sharing her experience.

"Flossie," she said, "you'll never guess what just happened to me; I got saved!" It was amusing to watch Flossie's face! It was evident that she was at a loss for words. She didn't know what to say. Finally, she mumbled out the words,

"That's nice, Billie," as she looked over at my dad. Her unspoken question was written on her face, "Has she lost it, Lewis; is this the beginning of the end?" I don't know if Flossie ever accepted Christ, but she sure did get witnessed to that day!

I drove back to Gainesville that afternoon and the car was filled with the joy that only comes from having led someone into a personal relationship with Jesus. But, I couldn't forget the face of my father, pushing me away when I tried to introduce him to my dearest Friend; and, I breathed yet another prayer for him.

Billie's physical condition worsened over the next couple of weeks and she was admitted to the hospice hospital in Jacksonville with little hope of ever coming out alive. Joy and I blocked out a Saturday to go to see her at the hospital. As we walked into the hospital room, my father was sitting beside her bed. He turned to look as we walked in the room. Without so much as a "Hello, how are you?" the first words out of his mouth were,

"Son, before you leave here today, I want to do what Billie did!"

"You mean you want to get saved?" I asked.

"Whatever you call it," he said, "I want what she's got!"

"Is now too soon?" I asked, trying not too sound too eager.

"As good a time as any," my dad answered.

We left Joy and Billie to visit in the hospital room and Dad and I made our way to the waiting room for some privacy. To my dismay, when we arrived at the waiting room it was packed with people and cigarette smoke hung low in the air (pre-Clean Air Act days.) There was not a seat in the entire room! Anger with Satan welled up inside my heart. "Satan, you miserable wretched creature," I said, "You will not steal this moment from me. I have prayed too long for my father's salvation, and you will not steal it from me. In the name of Jesus, I command you to leave this room and take all these people with you!" Within 5 minutes time, every person in that room had gone and the atmosphere had cleared! Dad and I sat down in one corner of the room and I had the privilege of leading my own father into the family of God. We returned to the room to rejoin Joy and Billie and, for the first time ever, we were a family!

Billie's time was growing short and it was necessary for some family member to be with her around the clock. Joy volunteered to sit with her on Saturday night while I went back home to preach my Sunday sermon. Throughout the night Billie struggled to breathe as the cancer drained the life out of her lungs. Joy began to sing some of the old, familiar hymns to Billie. When she started out on the familiar refrain of "Amazing Grace, how sweet the sound that saved a wretch like me," she heard Billie's weak, frail voice join in, "I once was lost, but now, I'm found, was blind, but now I see!" A little while later, she went home to be with her new-found Lord." A few days later, it was my joy and privilege to perform her funeral service.

My father started attending a little church in his community. Unfortunately, it was a church torn by internal power struggles between two different factions. Both sides saw a potential ally in my father and they began to recruit him into their political struggle. My father wanted nothing to do with that, so he just stopped attending the services so he wouldn't have to contend with their recruitments. I could hardly blame him, but I was disappointed that he was no longer going to church.

Despite his lack of church attendance, it was evident that something had happened in his life. He stopped smoking and cut way back on his drinking that had been such a major part of his life up to that point. He stopped hanging out at the local tavern and spent most of his time at home. But, the biggest change that was evident to us was his change of attitude. The gruff man that we had known all our lives became a gentle, loving dad. There was no way he could make up for not being there for us in our younger years, but he sure did try! He even started making frequent Sunday drives down to Gainesville to be with us in our Sunday morning service. We would have lunch together and then he would drive back home that afternoon. When he got too old to drive, he recruited my cousin Helen to drive him.

Some years passed and one day Dad noticed a lesion on the back of his tongue. A visit to the doctor and a subsequent biopsy revealed that my father had also developed cancer on his tongue. The doctors told us that this was a secondary cancer that had spread from somewhere else in his body, but they were unsuccessful in determining exactly where it had come from. The cancer spread rather rapidly and soon Dad was also under hospice's care, awaiting the inevitable end. The doctor's advised us children that he had about two weeks left to live.

All of us were saddened by the doctor's diagnosis. But, my biggest concern was not his physical welfare; I wanted to be reassured about his spiritual condition. My dilemma was how to ask him about it without conveying to him that I doubted his salvation experience. If I could not be a part of the solution, I surely did not want to be a part of the problem.

I drove to Jacksonville to see him the next weekend. When I arrived at the hospital the room was filled with my sisters and their families. I didn't want to create an awkward scene with them there, but I had to have an answer. I leaned over the bed and gave Dad a gentle hug as we entered the room. I cleared my throat, breathed a silent prayer for help, and began.

"Well, Dad, what are the doctors saying to you?" I began.

"You want to know what I think Son?" he asked. "I think I've got maybe six months to a year to live." I knew he didn't have that long, but I didn't want to be the one to tell him so.

"Well, how does that make you feel?" I asked.

"Well, considering the life I've lived, I've had a pretty good life," he said, "I don't think I have any complaints."

"Well, are you afraid?" I asked, pressing the issue of his readiness.

"Are you trying to get around to asking me if I'm ready to go to heaven?" he asked with a sly little grin on his face.

"Am I that obvious?" I asked in embarrassment.

"Pretty obvious, Son!" he replied, "and, I'm surprised that you would ask that, considering that you were there when it happened!"

"I'm sorry, Dad," I said, "I just want to make sure that you're ready for whatever happens."

"I'm OK, Son," he said, "I talk to the Lord every day; and sometimes He even talks back to me. I'm ready for whatever happens."

Relief swept over me and my emotions got the best of me. I choked up and began to cry. Through my tears I said,

"Dad, it just seems so unfair; we've never had much of a father-son relationship and now when we've developed this new relationship as brothers in Christ, we have so little time to enjoy it!" My father gently looked at me and with wisdom far beyond his apparent immature faith in Christ, he said,

"We'll have all the time we need, Son, in a little while!" I hugged him again and rejoiced that God had given me the assurance I was looking for.

My father had made but one request of us; he wanted his three children and our adopted sister, Ann to be present when he died. In the providence of God, the four of us were there on the night the Lord took him home to heaven. As the time drew near, the hospice nurse told us that it was only a matter of minutes. Dad was in and out of sleep. In one of his waking moments, I leaned over his bed and looked into his eyes. "Dad," I said, "in a few minutes the angels will be coming to get you and take you home. I just want you to know that we all are ready for that, and it's OK with us for you to go. Go in peace and we will join you later." He closed his eyes and never opened them again.

A few days later, I preached his funeral sermon. As much as I had grown to love him, his death was a beautiful experience. The peace that I had in knowing he was ready to go outweighed the grief I felt at his passing. I released him into the hands of a loving God, knowing that he was ready to go. My father had lived a hard-drinking, sinful life and most of it was wasted years. But, he had turned to God and God forgave him; he was a trophy of God's unlimited grace!

Chapter Six

A Felon In The Family

THE PHONE CALL

The urgent sounding phone awakened us at 4:30 in the morning. It was Monday, April 1, 1986, April Fool's day, exactly seven years to the day that we had rolled into Gainesville, Florida to assume the pastorate of the First Assembly of God. I wish it had been an April Fool's joke, but the tearful voice on the other end of the line let me know that this was no joke.

"Dad," he said, "I've just made the stupidest mistake I've ever made in my life!" The voice was our middle son, Steven.

"What is it son? What's happened? Where are you?" the three questions fell in rapid-fire order from my lips.

"I'm in the Forsyth County jail in Winston-Salem, North Carolina," he said, "I committed an armed robbery and they caught me."

"We'll be there as soon as we can get there," I said, and hung up the phone. My wife was already awake and had been listening on the speakerphone. We got up, threw our clothes into a suitcase and headed out for the 9-hour drive to Winston-Salem.

STEVEN'S GROWING-UP YEARS

Steven was our third son and the middle one in birth order. He had attended Georgia Southwestern College in Americus, Georgia and had developed an excellent work ethic at an early age. He even managed to purchase his own home at the tender young age of 19 in a nice residential part of Americus. He married his teen-age sweetheart who attended our church in that city. As far as we knew, both of them were living a Christian life and going to church regularly. But, we were 250 miles away in Gainesville, Florida, happily pastoring our church and totally ignorant of what was going on in their lives. His good work ethic soon landed him a lucrative job with a tobacco company in North Carolina. He was given a company car, an expense account, a list of clients on whom to call, and a gun permit to protect the large sums of money he would sometimes carry on his person. He soon built his savings account to $10,000 and his wife enrolled in King's College to work on her last year toward a teaching certificate. I didn't like the fact that he worked for a tobacco company, but he was, after all, 27 years old and capable of making his own decisions. They settled in to their comfortable lifestyle in Charlotte, N.C. Everything was right in their little world; but, not with God!

When we would ask about their church attendance, they would always tell us that they were still shopping around trying to find the right church where they could fit in. They assured us that everything was OK and that we were not to worry about them. I so wanted them to live for God that I chose to believe the lies they were telling me. But, not Joy; her mother's intuition told her that something was wrong with Steven. She was often awakened in her sleep with promptings from the Holy Spirit to pray for Steven. On one occasion she even called him at daybreak to find out if he was alright. On the other end of the line he assured her that everything was just fine. But, he couldn't escape the "coincidence" that even while he was talking to her on the phone, a friend was picking the buckshot out of his back with tweezers. A store owner had interrupted their burglary in the middle of the night and fired a round at Steven as he was diving through the window to escape. But, even that "coincidence" of his mother's call did not deter him from the life of crime that he had chosen.

A combination of factors had shaped our son's lives. In their growing-up years we did not have much money to spend on life's luxuries. We did travel a lot and they got to see a lot of America. But, even then, the only way we could afford to do that was to camp. Fortunately, all of us but Mom were actively involved in Royal Rangers and we well knew how to set up and break down camp. We became quite familiar with America's national parks.

But, we also wanted our boys to appreciate the value of money and to develop a strong work ethic so they could make their way in life. We wanted them to be productive members of society and not to become "takers" who took more than they gave. When they became old enough to drive, we helped them get jobs and to buy a car, which they paid for themselves. They bought their own gas and insurance. When it was time for college, they got student loans and paid their own way. This was partly because we did not have money to fund the wants and needs of five sons; but, it was also partly because we wanted them to learn to be responsible for themselves. Today they all have become productive members of society, so I think it worked quite well.

STEVEN'S MIRACULOUS HEALING

Steven had been a good son who had successfully navigated the turbulent waters of being the middle son in five boys. For the most part, his early years were uneventful; just the normal processes of growing up in a pastor's home. He was literally our "miracle child." When he was six years old, we were pastoring the First Assembly of God in Thomasville, Georgia. Joy and I had to attend the District Council in Griffin, Georgia. I had chaired the Constitution and Bylaws Revision Committee and was deeply involved in the convention proceedings. Our neighbor, Sue Banks, the wife of one of our deacons had agreed to keep our boys while we were at the council meetings. Sue called us during the meetings to tell us that Steven had developed flu-like symptoms and the doctors had admitted him to the hospital. His condition did not appear to be life-threatening, and since I was so heavily involved in the council, we decided that Joy would take the bus to Thomasville and I would finish out the council. As soon as the council was over I drove home to Thomasville.

The doctors were tight-lipped about Steven's condition. I could not understand their reluctance to tell us anything. It was, after all, "just the flu" wasn't it? What I didn't know was that they didn't know either! They were trying to fit his symptoms into some kind of paradigm that they were familiar with. Their first diagnosis was, in fact, that he had influenza. When he did not respond to their treatment, they changed their diagnosis to "strep infection in the blood stream." They kept him in the hospital for two weeks during which time his condition did not improve. After two weeks of exasperation, I called the doctor to complain about their apparent complacency and lack of communication. Nothing could have prepared me for what I was about to hear.

"Reverend, it appears that your son's heart has been affected by the strep infection in his bloodstream. It has been so damaged that it is only beating at half its normal speed. He will be a cardiac invalid for the rest of his life. He will not be able to participate in strenuous activities and, absolutely no sports at all. You will have to protect him from any events that would excite him in any way. He will suffer frequent fainting spells, and from one of them he just won't wake up!"

"Are you telling me that my son is going to die?" I asked him.

"Well, I didn't want to put it that bluntly, but that's what it ultimately boils down to. We've done everything we know how to do. You can come get your son and take him home. We will dismiss him tomorrow morning," he said. Stunned and in shock, I hung up the phone. I turned to Joy and explained what the doctor had said. She has always been a woman of great faith and a tower of strength. Even so, I could not understand her peace at hearing such dire news of our son's death sentence.

It was Wednesday evening and we began to get ready for our midweek church service. When we arrived at church, we shared our sad news with our congregation. They didn't want to have a regular church service and suggested that we turn the entire evening into a prayer meeting for Steven. That's exactly what we did. For the next hour and a half we just prayed. At times we would pray as individuals; at other times we would pray in concert, all the while focusing our prayers on Steven's full recovery. We all left the prayer meeting hopeful, but I don't think any of us realized just how effective our prayers would be.

The next morning Joy and I went to the hospital to pick up our son. When we arrived at the room, our pediatrician was there to meet us.

"Could we step across to the conference room," he said, "I've got some good news for you!"

"I sure could use some good news," I said as he led the way into the conference room. We sat down and he began to tell us the best news we had ever heard.

"After our conversation last night, I called in another cardiologist to get his opinion. He has a different perspective on this situation. He thinks our original diagnosis was wrong. The strep infection has nothing to do with this heart abnormality. It appears that Steven was born without an AV node in his heart; he is only the 25th person in medical history to have this birth defect and none of us has ever encountered this before. But, the EKG's confirm his diagnosis."

"But, isn't the AV node what tells his heart when to beat?" I asked, "How does his heart know when to beat? What gives it that impetus?"

"None of us knows the answer to that question," he said, "but somewhere within his body there is generated an impulse that tells his heart when to beat."

"But, what about this cardiac invalid thing?" I asked. "Will we have to still shield him from any strenuous activities?"

"For all practical purposes, you can forget that you ever came to see us," he said, "He will lead a normal life. Just be aware that his heart will beat at half the normal speed for a person his age and size. But, don't be alarmed; for him that is normal!"

"Well, I know you have to believe your diagnostics, Doctor," I said, but I have a better explanation. My congregation met last night and bombarded heaven on Steven's behalf. God heard their prayers. He healed Steven and left Him with a reminder of his miracle in the half-speed heartbeat, just like He did with Jacob's limp in the Old Testament." The doctor smiled and closed his chart. A year or so later, he received the baptism of the Holy Spirit and became the pastor of a large charismatic congregation in Thomasville!

It was not until some time later that God gave me proof that my account of Steven's healing was the right one. If Steven had truly been born with a heart that beats at half the normal speed, why did NO pediatrician in six years ever pick up the abnormal heartbeat? Every doctor's visit always begins with the frigid stethoscope against the chest. Surely, some doctor in six years would have noted that his heart was not beating at the normal speed. It's been 40 years since that diagnosis and Steven's heart is still beating along at half the normal speed.

HIS SPIRITUAL TURNAROUND

However, just after his thirteenth year he developed another disease that proved to be nearly fatal—to his parents! It's called "fourteen!" After raising five sons through their teenage years, we are convinced that "fourteen" is, indeed a disease. We don't really know what happened to Steven that year. He was not actively rebellious. Each of the boys had chores to do around the house, and while they might have grumbled, they usually did them without too much fuss. Steven did his without verbal complaint; but, the look in his eyes was akin to pure hatred. I would see him taking the trash to the street and I could see seething resentment in his eyes. We never really knew what the source of the problem was. But, we sure were aware that it was there.

Going to youth camp was an annual tradition in our house and the boys always looked forward to going. It was a time of fun activities, getting reacquainted with old friends from years gone by, and making new friends. It was also a time of renewed dedication to God in the nightly altar services. It also gave us a time for some parental bonding, since Joy and I usually went along as camp counselors. That particular year, I was serving as the camp coordinator and responsible for leading the night services. As usual, the kids were getting into the altar services and each night intensified from the night before. For whatever reason however, Steven had determined not to get into the night services. Thursday night was the last altar service and Steven's friends from the church were determined that Steven was going to get what he needed from God. I purposely avoided him for fear that I might be a part of the problem. I just watched with keen interest—and prayed. Finally, I saw Steven begin to crumble. Soon, he was in tears in the altar crying out to God. And, that boy prayed through! As I watched and rejoiced from a distance, I so wanted to rush over and hug him and tell him how much I loved him and to tell him how happy I was for his rededication. But, I was afraid I might hinder what God was doing in his heart. I knew, however, that Steven would have to confront his resentment toward me before the matter could be completely settled with God. I waited—and prayed. In a few minutes, Steven got up from the altar, looked around the building to find where I was. He made a beeline toward me. He stopped about arm's length in front of me, unsure of what to say or do. Finally, he sobbed and said,

"I love you, Daddy!"

"I love you, Son!" We fell into each other's arms and wept away the anger and resentment.

Steven returned to the church a different boy. He would sit at his drum throne in church playing for the praise and worship service and the anointing of God was all over him. The joy of the Lord shined from his face. He played the drums with a new intensity and it was obvious that it was an act of worship on his part. We would hear shouts of "Hallelujah!" and "Praise the Lord!" throughout the service. Oftentimes, tears of joy would trickle down his cheeks as he played in honor of Jesus, his Lord and friend. That was the Steven I remembered when that 4:30 phone call came on April 1, 1986.

WE GO TO JAIL

The nine-hour drive to Winston-Salem seemed like the longest drive we had ever taken. We had called our staff to let them know what had happened and to let them know where we would be for that week. We swore them to secrecy. The church was planning a big celebration with dinner-on-the-grounds the next Sunday in honor of our 7th anniversary as their pastors. We did not want to spoil the festivities. And, we needed time to think about what we would do next.

If Steven had been arrested in Florida, I would have known what to do. I would have had attorney friends that I could have called. I would have had friends with influence that could have gone to bat for him. But, North Carolina? I didn't know anyone there; no attorneys, no judges, no one!

Late that afternoon we arrived at the Forsythe County jail in Winston-Salem, North Carolina. We were waiting in the lobby for permission to go back to see our son in the holding area. A young lady in a police uniform came up to us.

"Are you Rev. Lastinger?" she asked.

"Yes, I am," I reassured her. With deep compassion, she looked me in the eye and said,

"I am the arresting officer, sir, and I'm so sorry for what you are going through. I hate to tell you this. I know you think your son is a good boy who made a bad mistake, but I have to tell you that your son is a hardened criminal and this is not his first offense."

"I know that this is your job," I said, "and I assure you that I hold no animosity toward you; you did your job and you did it well. But, you are wrong, my son is no criminal; he is exactly what you said—a good boy who made a mistake!" She knew what I did not know—that the facts would prove her right; Steven was living a criminal lifestyle.

There has never been a time in my life, before or since, when I felt as helpless as I did when we walked into the holding area. It was nothing like what you see on television. There were no seats, no ping-pong like table where you sat across from each other. We were in a steel-plated room that looked like it had a thousand or more coats of paint. With nothing to absorb the sound, our voices reverberated around the room like an echo chamber. There was a single bullet-proof glass window pane in the wall and a telephone headset. On the other side of the glass I could see my son, his body shaking with sobs and fear, tears streaming down his face. I desperately wanted to reach out and put my arms around him and tell him I loved him. I wanted to tell him, "It'll be OK son, Daddy will fix it! We'll make it all right!" But, bullet-proof glass, a steel wall, and armed guards separated us. And, I knew that this time Daddy couldn't make it all right. We assured him of our love and support, talked about getting a lawyer, and suddenly our time was up. Tears were flowing freely on both sides of that wall.

The young policewoman was waiting in the lobby for us.

"Would you like a contact visit with your son, sir," she asked.

"Can you do that for us?" I asked.

"I think I can," she answered. She made a call and arranged to have him transferred to an interrogation room at the court house.

Only two people were allowed in to see him, so his wife and I went into the room. We hugged and cried together.

"Before anything else Son, I want to know about your relationship with the Lord," I said.

"I took care of that last night at 90 miles per hour flying down the Interstate with ten police cars in hot pursuit!" he said. "I promised God that if he got me out of this alive, I would live for him the rest of my life!" We weren't sure whether or not the interrogation room was "bugged" so our conversation was guarded at that point. However, from that meeting and subsequent conversations a sad and disappointing story began to unfold. Steven's life of crime had begun in his teenage years. It started with shoplifting. When he was successful in getting away with that, he began to seek more exciting challenges, finally resorting to breaking and entering and burglary. At the time of his arrest he was charged with three armed robberies of Food Lion supermarkets in the Winston-Salem area. He was guilty of two of them, but he was visiting family in Americus, Georgia at the time of the third crime.

OUR CHURCH RESPONDS

We finished out the week in Winston-Salem, tying up all the loose ends and making arrangements for the upcoming trial. We contacted an attorney and paid him his fee. Then, we headed out on that long journey back to Gainesville. We had to make a decision; "What do we tell our church; how much do they need to know? Do we really have to tell them anything at all? After all, they are 500 miles away." Joy and I are both very transparent people and our lives are an open book. The book that you are reading is a testimony to that fact. In the end, we decided to tell the church everything and let the chips fall wherever they may. We did not want to look into the eyes of our congregation and wonder what they knew. We did not want them to think we couldn't trust them with our saddest secret. Our only concern now was what to do about the anniversary celebration the following Sunday.

Sunday morning came and the festivities were in full swing. It was evident that our staff had kept the secret as they had promised. Nobody seemed to know anything. Joy and I put on our best plastic smiles and pretended nothing was wrong as we were presented with gifts for the seven years we had served as their pastors. At the conclusion of the service, I stepped to the pulpit and announced, "Today is a happy occasion and we are honored by your expressions of love. And, while this is a happy day, this has been the saddest week of our lives. The greatest tragedy we have ever experienced has struck our family. We don't want to dampen the joy of this festive occasion, so we are not going to get into the details of what has happened in this service. Enjoy your dinner-on-the-grounds; come back tonight and we will tell you the whole story. I will tell you this, however. I have not had an affair! Joy and I are not getting a divorce! And, I am not submitting my resignation as your pastor! I could hear audible sighs of relief in the congregation.

I don't think we had ever had such a large crowd at our Sunday night service as we had that night! Whether it was morbid curiosity or loving concern that drew them; you be the judge. I did not have it in me to preach a sermon. When we finished the praise and worship service, I simply stepped to the front on the main floor near the communion table. I took a hand-held microphone and began to unfold the story of what had happened that past week. Joy stood beside me and very soon our tears were flowing. Before I finished the story, a marvelous, mystical thing happened. Not en masse, but one-by-one the congregation got up out of their seats and began to come to the front to stand beside us and weep with us. Before it ended over 200 people were standing at the altar crying with us. There was nothing they could do; but, just being there with us was enough. It was the most beautiful expression of agape love that we have ever witnessed before or since.

After service one of the men in our church came to me and said,

"Pastor, when are we going to get our boy?"

"What do you mean, Dick?" I asked.

"Well, we can't let him sit there in the jail cell all alone, Pastor!" he replied.

"But Dick, his bail is set at $100,000; it would take $15,000 non-refundable bond to get him out. He would only be out three weeks before he has to appear for trial and he will surely be sent to prison. It's not worth it for just three weeks; and, besides I don't have that kind of money!" I said.

"Well, I do!" he said, "And you can say it's not worth it because you're not the one sitting there in that jail cell!"

"I can't let you do that, Dick. He'll just have to stay there. The matter is settled."

Dick had been the owner of a small aluminum installation company when I first met him. He and his crew were installing sound paneling in our church to improve the acoustics. As they were putting up the paneling, I was singing to the accompaniment of sound tracks through the P.A. system. Dick got so under conviction that he came to church the following Sunday and gave his heart to the Lord. God blessed his business and he expanded into commercial construction and became a wealthy man.

The next morning when I arrived at church Dick was waiting with airline tickets in hand.

"I've got the money in my pocket; let's go!" he said.

"Dick, I told you not to do that," I said.

"I know what you said, but it's my money and I did it anyway. Now, let's go before we miss our plane!" He wouldn't take "No" for an answer, so I called Joy to tell her where we were going, then got in the car with Dick and headed for the airport. He had bought first-class tickets there and back.

In Winston-Salem we went straight to the attorney's office to make the arrangements. He took us to a bail-bondsman who would put up the money for Steven's bail. The attorney negotiated a better percentage for us and we ended up paying $10,000 for Steven's bond. Dick reached in his pocket and counted out $10,000 into the bail-bondsman's hands. The bail-bondsman disappeared with the money and headed for the jail to pick up Steven. In a little while Steven came walking down the sidewalk surrounded by four of the biggest giants I have ever seen! I believe those guys invented steroids! The attorney painted a grisly picture of what Steven would look like if he jumped bail and those guys had to hunt him down. Steven had not thought of skipping bail, but if the thought had ever occurred to him I'm sure that visual picture would have changed his mind. Our commercial flight had already left without us when we got to the airport. Dick chartered a pilot and a Beechcraft Bonanza to fly us to Gainesville. Dick had been a friend before Steven's arrest, but he certainly proved his friendship during that terrible ordeal.

THE TRIAL

We have never contended that Steven was innocent, or that he should not go to prison. He committed a crime and he deserved to do the time. However, we did learn that the term "justice system" is an oxymoron. The man with the money and influence walks; the rest go to prison. In my opinion, the attorney who was referred to us was only interested in our money; he did not have Steven's best interest at heart. He was a golfing buddy of the District Attorney who happened to be up for re-election the following month. The case made big headlines in the North Carolina press and Steven was dubbed "the Interstate Bandit." The D.A. intended to ride the case to victory in his bid for re-election. We believe the case was settled on the golf course before it ever went to court. Our attorney painted a bleak picture of how our case would go down. "They will try your three counts as three different cases," he said. "You'll get 20 years for the case in which you were caught red-handed. Then, they'll try you on the next case where you were caught on videotape. You'll get 20 more years for that! Then, they'll try you on the third case as a convicted felon and a two-time loser, and you'll get at least 20 more years for that! By the time this is over, you could be in prison for the rest of your life!" His advice was to plead "No Contest" and throw yourself on the mercy of the court. Reluctantly, Steven decided to take his advice.

28 days later we sat in a courtroom not knowing what to expect. The D.A. decided to group the three counts together in one case. We listened silently as the prosecuting attorney presented his evidence against Steven. The detectives had done their work well and they presented a very convincing case. There was nothing to be said in Steven's defense. When they came to the third case however, we knew Steven was innocent. What we did not know, however, was that when you plead "No Contest" you are not allowed to speak in your own defense. When I protested that Steven was not even in North Carolina at the time of the third robbery, our attorney came

unglued. I don't know what he was so excited about, but he had neglected to tell us that we were not supposed to speak. I sat down and the prosecutor concluded his case.

"Young man, this court has no choice but to find you guilty as charged. Do you have anything you would like to say before I pass sentence?" the judge asked. Steven stood to his feet and with trembling lips he began.

"I can say nothing in my defense, Your Honor. I have committed some terrible crimes. I have sinned against the state of North Carolina, against my victims, against my parents, and most of all, against my God. I am ashamed that I have let my parents down; they are not to blame for what I have done. They brought me up right; they taught me right from wrong. I alone am to blame for the choices I have made." By now, all our tears were flowing heavily and Steven was talking through his sobs. Even the woman bailiff was wiping tears from her eyes. "I have no right to ask for mercy Your Honor. What I have done deserves punishment. I can only promise you that this will never happen again. I will not fail my family or my God again. I plead for your mercy in the sentence you give me." The judge took out his handkerchief, wiped the tears from his eyes, and said,

"I find the defendant, Steven Lastinger, guilty of three counts of armed robbery and hereby sentence him to 20 years, seven of which are mandatory, to be served in the North Carolina prison system." He banged the gavel down and dismissed the court.

The case was closed; our attorney smiled all the way to the bank, and Steven settled in for the longest seven years of his life. It was only a small consolation that the District Attorney lost his bid for re-election the following week. Our attorney will have to wait until eternity to get his reward.

THE PRISON YEARS

The first year of Steven's imprisonment was the worst. The shock of prison life was overwhelming to him and even to us. Joy and I could not bear to look at movies with prison scenes in them. He needed some dental work done which required that he be sent to the main prison in North Carolina—the place where all the really bad guys are incarcerated. On one occasion, Steven even saw one of the prisoners murder a fellow prisoner with a homemade knife. If he had revealed what he saw it would have put his own life in jeopardy.

We all still had hopes that somehow we could get an appeal to at least get his sentenced reduced. After all, this was his first arrest. We were contacted by a man who worked for the prison system and claimed to be an advocate for the inmates. He said that he needed money to get the wheels of progress working to get Steven's sentence reduced. We paid him $1200, believing we could trust him since he was an employee of the prison system. As it turned out, he was arrested as a con artist and ended up going to prison himself. And, of course, our money was gone for good.

The pain of Steven's first year in prison was intensified as he helplessly watched his marriage crumble and fall apart. A few months after he was sentenced, his wife informed him that she was pregnant with another man's child and that she was divorcing him. His divorce papers arrived on Christmas day, almost exactly eight months after he had been sentenced.

At the end of the first year, Steven gave up any hope of getting a reduced sentence. He told us, "I did the time; I'll just do my time and get it over with. I'm here for the long haul and I'll just make the best of it." Reluctantly, his mother and I agreed.

Our oldest son, Allen had once worked as a prison guard in the state of Florida. "Dad," he said, "Steven can live a Christian life in prison, but it won't be the kind of Christian life you visualize. If he displays weakness they will trample all over him. He will have to stake out his territory and perhaps even defend it before they will leave him alone." Allen's words proved to be prophetic. More than once, Steven had to defend himself and his faith in prison. He began working out daily and grew facial hair in order to intimidate anyone who entertained thoughts of running over him. It must have worked because they soon left him alone and he was able to live in a state of relative peace in that hostile world.

The qualities that it took to live a Christian life in prison also made him an ideal prisoner. Steven soon worked his way up to honor status and was transferred to a medium-security prison in Yadkinville, N.C. A little, elderly woman named Lena Caudle conducted a weekly prison ministry at the prison when she came and ministered to the inmates. Steven joined her group and she lovingly adopted him as "one of her boys." She became his spiritual mentor and advisor during his stay in Yadkinville. He became interested in playing the piano and she taught him what she knew. One of the men in our church, Buddy Morrison, heard of Steven's interest in music; he bought him an electronic keyboard and personally delivered it to him in Yadkinville. With plenty of time on his hands, Steven became quite proficient on the electric keyboard. He also became an accomplished harmonica player.

In time, good behavior earned Steven a minimum-security status and he was transferred to Spindale, N.C. At Spindale, inmates were allowed to get jobs in the community. It was good for everybody. The inmates were able to build up a bank account, the employers got dependable employees, and the prison system charged $300 a month rent on the prisoner's jail cells. Everybody wins! Steven's good work ethic acquired during his younger years served him well while he was in prison. He soon was promoted to production supervisor in the plant where he worked. And, all the while, his bank account kept growing.

Even with his full-time job, Steven still had time on his hands. The State of North Carolina would pay for an inmate's Associate's degree in the local community college and even provide transportation if needed. Steven enrolled and successfully completed the two-year program while still holding down a full-time job in the marketplace. And, all the while his bank account kept growing. After graduation, he decided to go on to get his Bachelor of Science degree at the local four-year college. The state would not pay for that, so he dipped into his own savings to pay his tuition and books. They also would not provide his transportation, so he had to arrange a ride to school and back each day. He completed his B.S. program and graduated with honors while still serving time in the N.C. penal system.

One of the instructors at the Spindale prison was the pastor of the First Assembly of God in Spindale. He befriended Steven and would pick him up on Sunday morning to play the keyboard for the church worship team. It was there that he met Angela Tate, the girl who would one day become his wife. Word of Steven's keyboard talent spread throughout the small community and the local Methodist pastor contacted him about becoming his Minister of Music. Steven tried it out for a few weeks, but there was one little, old lady in the choir that didn't particularly like him. She complained that his songs weren't "Methodist" enough. When the pastor invited Steven to accept the position, Steven told him that he would only accept if 100% of the choir approved the choice. To his surprise, even the little, old lady voted to take the young Pentecostal boy on board. They would pick him up from the prison on Sunday morning to play at the Methodist church. The service ended early enough that they could shuttle him over to the First Assembly of God and he could play for their service as well! The pastor would take him to lunch and then drop him off back at the prison.

His romance with Angela deepened with the passing of time. Even though he was still in prison, he asked her to be his wife and she accepted. On Thanksgiving Eve, Nov. 22, 1989, Joy and I drove to North Carolina, checked him out of prison and performed the wedding ceremony at the First Assembly of God in Spindale. His pass privilege at the prison required that he not be out of our custody at any time; so, that same night we drove to our timeshare condo in Banner Elk, N.C. Steven and Angela spent their wedding night and their honeymoon with all the family in our condo in the N.C. mountains. When his week-end pass expired, we checked him back into prison and took Angela back home to await his release.

That release came on May 20, 1993, seven years and one day from the date he was sentenced. His good behavior earned him an unconditional release without the need for parole or any kind of supervisory follow-up.

EPILOGUE

It has been said that "the best lessons are bought lessons!" The lesson Steven learned from his life of crime was an expensive lesson—he paid dearly. But, he learned his lesson well. Upon his release from prison he took a minimum-wage job as a dump-truck driver. Meanwhile, he put his newly-acquired computer skills to work writing a program for a local manufacturing company. The owner was so impressed that he offered Steven a job and he could name his own salary. He had been out of touch with the world of commerce and he priced himself too low, but, at least he had a good job doing what he loved to do. In time, he graduated on to more lucrative positions with other companies.

Today, Steven, Angela and their daughter, Caroline live in Florida where he is an automobile insurance appraiser and automobile body shop manager. They are actively serving God and attending church regularly. He tithes faithfully and God has blessed his obedience with a good job and a beautiful home. Like the Old Testament Joseph, "what Satan intended for evil, God has turned for good."

Chapter Seven
Tragedy Strikes The Lastingers

"Ginger Dixon Lastinger—Our Sweetheart"

A ringing phone after bedtime is never a welcome sound. It was 11:30 and the concerned voice on the other end of the line was our Associate Pastor, Terry Fulton. His wife, Lynn was the sister of our oldest son's wife, Ginger.

"Something terrible has happened to Ginger," Terry said, "And I don't know all the details. I'm sure Allen will be calling you."

"Thanks, Terry." I mumbled into the phone and hung up to await Allen's call. In a few minutes, the phone rang again and I heard the tearful voice on the other end of the line,

"Dad, Ginger's dead! My wife is gone!"

"No, son, surely there has been some mistake! What happened?" I asked.

"We went to bed about 10:30 and she fell off to sleep." he said, "I stayed awake to read a while. About 11:00 I heard a gurgling noise coming from her throat and tried to awaken her, but she wouldn't respond. I tried CPR but it didn't help. I called 911 and they came as quickly as possible, but they weren't able to resuscitate her either. They pronounced her dead on the scene and they've taken her for an autopsy."

"I'll be there as quickly as we can get there, son!" I said, and hung up the phone.

Through teary eyes, Joy and I got dressed, threw a few clothes into an overnight bag, called our other sons, and headed for the car. Lakeland, Florida is just two hours south of Gainesville. We both wept silently as we drove through the deep, dark, murky midnight of February 9, 1994. I had never felt as wrapped in sorrow as we did on that trip to Lakeland.

Allen greeted us at the door when we arrived. His two daughters, Sarah, age nine and Rachel, age seven were mercifully asleep when their mother went home to be with Jesus. Allen had obviously been crying when we arrived. There wasn't much to be said. She was gone and we were all feeling the same sorrow. I cannot imagine the anguish Allen must have been feeling, and I would certainly never try to minimize that pain in any way. But, please try to understand why I feel that perhaps my load was the heaviest load of all. My fatherly heart was aching for the loss my son was experiencing. I would have given anything to be able to relieve his pain. And, I felt that I needed to be strong for my wife—I knew how much she loved Ginger too. The two little girls would need a pillar of strength they could lean on, and Grandpa desperately wanted to be that strong pillar. Ginger had been an integral part of our church family in Gainesville and I knew our congregation would be looking to me for answers—answers that I was also seeking for myself. I needed to be able to make sense of this tragedy for their sakes. Added to that was my own grief for the daughter I never had, the apple of my eye, my precious Ginger. The load was almost more than I could bear.

When the dawn broke, Allen went to do what no father should ever have to do. He first awakened Sarah to tell her that her mother had died during the night. I heard their muffled sobs and I knew Sarah had buried her face in her father's chest trying to cope with her loss and the fact that her mother would never be there to tuck her in at night again. Never again would her mother say her prayers with her before bedtime. In a little while, she came out of the room and sat down beside me on the couch. She looked up at me and smiled a weak smile, as if that was what she was expected to do.

"Honey, It's OK to cry whenever you feel like crying," I said to her. Her face clouded and she looked deeply into my eyes,

"If I did that Grandpa," she said, "I'd be crying all the time." That morning that little 9-year old girl gave up her childhood to become "Mom" to her little sister. She assumed a responsibility that no little girl should ever have to assume.

In a few minutes, Allen went into Rachel's room to awaken her. Again, the only sounds we could hear were muffled sobs coming from behind the closed doors. After a while alone together, Allen and Rachel came out of the bedroom and sat on the couch, she straddling his lap and leaning upon his chest. In a few minutes she sat upright with a wrinkled brow and said, "Daddy, what are we going to do for a Mommy now?" I couldn't hold it together any longer; I turned my head away to hide my tears and walked away from the sad scene.

Late that afternoon we drove back home to Gainesville, arriving after dark. We had been without sleep now for almost 36 hours and we were exhausted. We fell into bed and tried to sleep. I was awakened early the next morning by the sounds of different voices in the kitchen. Jerry and Dawn Lahman, one of our deacons and very dear friends, had taken the day off from work to come and serve us for the day. They cooked and cleaned, answered the many phone calls, and entertained the 100 or more people who came by to visit us that day. The Lahman's were executives with the local Burger King chain, but they taught us a lesson in servant-leadership that day. They were there when we needed them, and we will never forget what they did for us during that sorrow-filled time. Though our paths have taken us separate ways, we are very dear friends to this very day.

Allen, Ginger and the girls had been stationed in Brussels, Belgium in the military. While they were there they attended the International Assembly of God, an English-speaking congregation in Brussels. They became fast friends with AG missionaries David and Jimmie Ruth Lee, who were at that time the directors of International Media Ministries. Allen volunteered several hours per day to work with them developing ministry videos for distribution around the world. Allen and Ginger fell in love with missions and decided that they wanted to come home, finish their Bible College education and return to Europe as Media Missionaries. That is how they came to be in Lakeland at the time of Ginger's death. Allen was working on staff at the Carpenter's Home Church and finishing up his degree program at Southeastern College (now Southeastern University.) Their love for missions and their desire to return to Europe made Ginger's death even more difficult to understand.

In the midst of my grief, I was grappling with a wide range of other emotions as well. My most prevalent feelings were feelings of anger. I was very angry with God. I couldn't understand why He would let this happen to someone like Ginger. "Why God?" I wanted to scream at Him, "There are so many mean, wretched, cruel people in the world. Why didn't you take one of them and leave Ginger to go where she was going? Why would you leave two little girls without a mother to tuck them in at night and say their prayers? Why, God, why?" Well-intentioned friends would tell me, "God didn't do this, Satan did. God gives life, Satan takes it away!" I knew they were trying to ease my pain, but it only made me mad! Only my sense of propriety kept me from screaming at them, "Are you telling me that Satan is more powerful than God—that God couldn't have stopped Satan? Any way you slice it, God is still responsible!?" I felt like a little boy who didn't get his way, pounding on his father's chest, screaming "I hate you, I hate you!" while all the time wanting Him to hold me close and comfort my pain.

Intuitively, I knew that my congregation was grappling with the same issues and questions I was grappling with. I felt like I needed to have answers for them. Although Allen's boss, Pastor Karl Strader was going to do Ginger's funeral, I asked Allen if I could say a word, and he agreed. I was as open and transparent with my congregation then as I have been with you now. I told them of my anger and my frustration with God. I confessed to them that I had not yet found any answers to my questions. "But," I said, "If you think for one minute that I am abandoning my faith in God, you are wrong! If God does not have an answer to the senselessness of Ginger's death, then who does? God is sovereign and He can do whatever He chooses without asking my permission or explaining His reasoning to me. My challenge and my choice is to trust Him even when I do not understand why He is doing what He is doing!" I think many minds were settled that day; but, I confess to you that 14 years later I still do not have answers to why Ginger died. But, I'm still trusting God.

Chapter Eight
I Left Her Standing At The Station

Although Joy and I had traveled throughout Europe on several occasions, it was one of our favorite places to visit, and we especially enjoy sharing it with someone else. In the mid 1990's, when I found out that my sister and her husband would like to see Europe, Joy and I were quick to volunteer to serve as tour guides. Judy had never seen Europe and Bill had only been to Rome with his family as a young man. Neither of them were seasoned travelers and neither spoke any foreign language. They would very definitely be lost in a strange land, unable to speak the local language. They only agreed to go on vacation to Europe with us because I could speak French and we had traveled this area before.

Bill and Judy wanted to go on ahead to visit some of his family in Rome. Not much room for problems there; they would be met at the airport and grandly hosted as only the Italians can while they were in Rome. Bill's family would put them on the train from Rome to Marseille, France. Joy and I would fly from Atlanta to Barcelona, rent a car and drive to Marseille where we would join Bill and Judy for the rest of a three-week trip through Europe. We booked our tickets accordingly and made arrangements to meet at midnight at the train station in Marseille. Bill and Judy confidently headed off across the Atlantic to meet his family.

Joy and I finished our packing and got ready to leave a few days later. Effective flea treatment for dogs had not yet come into existence and our old Basset hound was on her last legs, terribly arthritic and terminally afflicted with fleas. Nothing we could do for her was working. She was so badly afflicted that she would lean against the wall of our garage and blood would run down the wall when she moved away. Our plan was to take her to a kennel while we were in Europe. Instead, on the day we were to depart, I found myself awakened at 5:00 a.m. having finally dreamed up enough courage to put the suffering old "Lady" out of her misery. I took my gun, dug a deep grave, and Lady died of "lead poisoning" that morning before daybreak. I don't regret what I did, it was an act of mercy; but, it didn't exactly start my day out right that morning.

I went in and awakened Joy to tell her what I had done. She didn't disapprove; she just couldn't believe her soft-hearted hubby could bring himself to do so a thing. Now that I think about it, I find it hard to believe I did it either! We got dressed, put our luggage in the car and headed for Atlanta to our son's house and on to Europe.

Our plan was to leave our car at David's house to have some touch-up work done on it and we would take the subway to the airport. "Dad, have Mom put your money in her bra before you leave," he said, "the subway is not a very safe place." That warning will take on special significance when you read the rest of this story. He took us and our luggage to the subway stop and dropped us off for the 45-minute ride to the airport. As we were dragging our luggage through the long terminal hallways at Hartsfield International Airport in Atlanta, I was grumbling about having to wait two hours for our airplane to depart.

We arrived at the ticket counter in plenty of time and were greeted cheerily by the ticket agent. As she checked our passports and travel documents, she looked up at me with a look of concern on her face and said,

"Sir, do you realize that your wife's passport expired four days ago?"

"Don't joke about a think like that," I said, not really thinking that there was anything to worry about. Surely, somebody could do something.

"Believe me sir, I'm not joking!" she said, with genuine concern on her face.

"Well, what do we need to do?" I said, "Surely, there is somebody we can contact. Maybe you can just let her fly and we will go to the consulate in Barcelona and get her a new passport."

"No sir," she replied, "If I let her fly, they will just turn her around and send her home on the next flight and we will be fined $1000 for letting her on board." She pointed to the phone bank across the terminal and said, "I don't know what to tell you sir, but there are the phones!" For the next two hours, I called every government office I knew to call. Not once in two hours did I get to talk to a real live human being! Every call I made was answered by an automatic answering system that told me to press 1, 2, 3, etc. Finally, in desperation, I called our son, David and explained our situation to him.

"Put Mom back on the subway, Dad, and send her to me. I'll meet her at the station and we'll do whatever we have to do to take care of this situation."

I have never felt the emotional anguish I felt at that moment. I could not stand the thought of leaving my wife in Atlanta while I flew off to vacation in Europe! At the same time, not going was not an option. I knew Bill and Judy were already enroute by train from Rome to Marseille and there was no way to contact them. They would be panic-stricken if they arrived at the Marseille train station at midnight and I was not there to meet them. They did not know how to convert money, could not speak French, and would have no idea what to do if I were not there for them. They were calling out the boarding call for the flight to Barcelona, and I didn't know what to do. I was so distraught that I was literally crying (not a very manly thing to do, I know!) Joy was urging me to go, telling me that she would catch up to me somewhere in Europe, but that I had to be there for Bill and Judy. Through teary eyes, I grabbed my carry-on luggage, kissed my wife good-bye and left her standing there in the terminal.

I had planned to sleep on the plane during the flight so I would be fresh for the drive from Barcelona to Marseille. If I did get sleepy, Joy would be there to help me. Needless to say, sleeping on that flight was out of the question! All through the night, I worked out Plan B, Plan C, and Plan D, all depending on when she would be able to join us in Europe. I arrived in Barcelona exhausted from the physical and emotional stress of the trip so far. Alone, I picked up the rental car and headed north on the road toward Marseille, France. I was so sleepy I know I was a danger to everyone on the highway. I kept slapping myself in the face to stay awake until I could get to Marseille. I finally arrived, located the train station and checked into a cheap hotel just a few blocks from the station. I managed to sleep for an hour or two before having to meet Bill and Judy at midnight. As expected, they were there blissfully ignorant of the drama that had unfolded without their knowledge while they enjoyed the beauty of the French Riviera passing by outside the train windows.

Back home, another drama was unfolding even without my knowledge. It can take up to six weeks to get a passport through normal means. Even an expedited passport takes a week. True to his word, while Mom was on the train back to his house, David was on the phone calling in every favor he could. He called his congressman, who referred him to our congressman in Florida. She gave him the number to call at the National Passport Center in Miami. By this time, it was after hours and he really did not expect to get an answer. A casual voice on the other end of the line answered, "Hello!" David explained our quandary to the woman who listened patiently. "Sir, our office is closed for the day," she explained, "I am the director and I just happened to be working overtime. I am probably the only person who can meet your request. You got the right person! If you will get two passport photos made and enclose them with the old passport; send them to me by overnight courier, I will personally walk them through the process tomorrow and overnight them to you tomorrow night. You will have them by 10:00 Wednesday morning." David picked up his mother at the train station, took her to get passport photos made, and overnighted them to Miami. True to her word, she had the passports back in Joy's hands by 10:00 Wednesday morning. At 11:30 Joy was on the plane headed for Genoa, Italy.

Meanwhile, in Europe Bill, Judy and I were driving along the coast of the Mediterranean headed for Italy. One of my alternate plans had called for us to pick Joy up in Genoa, Italy. While our original plans had disintegrated horribly, this plan worked perfectly. We arrived at the Genoa airport about 8:30 in the morning. Like a scene out of an old romantic Bogart-Bacall movie, we found Joy sitting on her luggage in the arrival terminal of the airport. I've never seen a more beautiful sight in my life! The scoundrel Romeo who had abandoned his trusting Juliet at the Atlanta airport was, at last, reunited with the love of his life.

The next three weeks took us to Venice, to the castles of Bavaria, and to Langenaltheim, Germany, the land of the Lastinger heritage. From there we drove southwest through Austria, over the Alps into Interlaken, Switzerland. The trip across the Alps is breathtaking at any time. As we approached the little village of Oberalpenpasse, the crest of the Alps, the snow was coming down pretty furiously. Natives of Florida, Bill and Judy had little experience with snow, and Judy was beside herself marveling at the beauty of the sea of white outside. We stopped at the top to make snowballs to throw at each other. Suddenly, from out of nowhere, a car appeared coming from the other direction. They pulled alongside us and rolled down the window.

"Can you tell us where the glacier is?" they asked.

"I'm sorry but we're tourists too," I yelled back. Concerned that the snow may make road closures necessary, we got into our car and proceeded on down the mountain toward Interlaken. In less than 5 minutes, we rounded a turn in the road and stared into the face of a huge, blue glacier visible through the falling snow. We would have missed it if we had not been alerted to its presence by some lost tourists who had driven right by it without seeing it. After taking pictures, we headed on down the mountain and watched the police close the highway behind us as we passed. The snow was getting too treacherous to drive in. We arrived in the beautiful town of Interlaken and checked into out hotel for the night.

From Interlaken, we drove north to Brussels, Belgium to visit our friends, David and Jimmie Ruth Lee, missionaries at International Media Ministries in Brussels. We all decided to go to dinner at a local restaurant and David invited us to go in his Speed-the-Light van so we could all be together. The van was one of the older models where the front doorpost makes a wicked 90-degree turn toward its hinges. As I jumped up into the right front seat, my right knee made solid contact with that immobile doorpost. A pain like liquid fire shot up and down my leg. It hurt so bad that I wanted to cry; only my warped sense of machismo prevented me from doing so. I rubbed and rubbed until finally the pain became bearable. Nothing appeared to be broken. Little did I know that the real injury was more subtle than that.

The last week of our 3-week vacation in Europe was to be spent in a timeshare condo on the Costa del Sol, the Mediterranean coast of Spain. We left Brussels, spent a couple of days in Paris, and drove south toward Spain. On the way, my back began to ache. I chalked it up to too much time spent sitting in the car. I took something to dull the pain and continued driving toward Spain. By the time we arrived in Spain, the pain had gotten worse. Still convinced that it was a back problem, Joy took the steam iron in the condo and literally ironed my back in an effort to relieve the pain. But, her heat therapy failed and the pain got worse. Wearing clothing became a problem. Everywhere the cloth touched my skin it would send shots of pain into my body. I found myself walking carefully around the condo with only a loose-fitting swimsuit on. Bill, Judy and Joy enjoyed as many of the local sights as they could, while I sat in the condo feeling sorry for myself.

On one of my few excursions outside the apartment, we went to a local restaurant to sample some of the local cuisine. Paella Maritima is a popular rice dish prepared in a deep pan with all kinds of seafood on it, including mussels, shrimp, scallops, crab, fish, squid, etc. When it arrived, everyone in the restaurant could have smelled it. It was the fishiest smelling dish I had every seen! I'm not into seafood at its best, and there was no way I was going to put any of that in my mouth. Judy, Bill, and Joy had intended to split the dish between them. I don't remember what I ordered, but I'll guarantee you it was not fish. Judy and Joy ended up eating from my plate. There was no way Bill was going to let the paella go to waste and he ended up eating the whole thing! Nobody got any sleep that night; Bill was up all night, sick from the "seafood overdose."

My miserable week finally came to an end and we headed toward the airport in Barcelona. Still believing that I was having a back problem, I tried to get as comfortable as I could on the flight home. To this day, I don't know what triggered the thought in my brain, but I turned to Joy and said, "You know, I'll bet I've got Shingles!" I'd never known anyone who had Shingles and I knew nothing about the symptoms of the disease. I just had this overwhelming impression that I had Shingles.

When we arrived back in Gainesville I called our family doctor and set up an appointment. Then, I went to work finding out as much as I could about the disease called Shingles. Armed with that information, I arrived at the doctor's office with a sheaf of printouts.

"What seems to be the problem?" he asked.

"I think I've got shingles!" I announced. He examined me, did a few tests, and then said,

"I think you're right; you've got a mild case of Shingles!" Mild? Mild? Did he say "mild?" Here I had been writhing in agony and he called it "Mild!" I discovered a great truth that day, a mild case is a disease the "other guy" has; only when it's your disease is it "serious." His treatment worked, however. In a few weeks the lesions healed, and the pain went away. The disastrous vacation in Spain became a fading memory.

Chapter Nine
Revival Fire In Gainesville

It was Wednesday morning in early 1993 and our church staff was busily engaged in planning all the things that are involved in running a growing church. In the middle of our staff meeting, my phone rang and I answered. It was one of our neighboring pastors calling to share with me some interesting news. The voice on the other end of the line was surging with excitement.

"Have you heard about what's happening at Carpenter's Home?" (A large Assembly of God church in Lakeland, Florida.)

"Something's always happening at Carpenter's Home!" I laughingly replied, "What are you talking about now?"

"They're having a supernatural, knock down, drag out revival!" he said. "People falling out on the floor all over the building; hundreds of people laughing with 'Holy Ghost laughter', it's the craziest thing you've ever seen! Some guy from South Africa named Rodney Howard Browne is the evangelist."

In my many years of ministry, I had seen quite a few visitations of God's Spirit on a congregation, but never had I seen anything like what he was describing to me. I was more than mildly intrigued by the possibilities. Looking at the rest of my staff, I said,

"Would you like to go and see for yourselves what he's talking about? I could get someone to cover the service for us tonight and we could drive down to Carpenter's Home Church in time for the evening service. Our collective curiosity got the best of us and in a couple of hours we were in a car headed for Lakeland, Florida.

The parking lot of the huge mega-church was nearly full and the building was filling up fast when we arrived. Even so, we were able to get a seat on the main floor in the middle about half way back in the huge 10,000-seat auditorium. We settled in and tried to be as inconspicuous as we could be.

From the very beginning, the service had an unusual air about it. Even before it began, isolated individuals would break out in laughter all over the auditorium. However, it was not too distracting and we were able to focus on what was going on at the front. The praise and worship was wonderful. In a large church there is so much talent that all the music usually sounds good. However, there is something unmistakable about music that is anointed of the Holy Spirit. And, this music was definitely anointed!

At an appropriate time in the service, the pastor recognized distinguished guests who were in the service. One well-known international singing evangelist was introduced and made his way to the platform to be recognized. He never made it; the nearer he got to the front, the "drunker" he became. By the time he reached the altar, he had fallen into a heap and was convulsing with laughter. A pastor from nearby Tampa came to the pulpit to testify of what had happened to his wife during the revival. He wanted nothing to do with what he thought was just some momentary theological madness, so his wife went to the revival without him. When midnight came and she was still not home, he began to worry about her. Finally, about 2:00 she came in and her face was radiant. Her eyes were sparkling and every time she tried to tell him about the service she broke into spasms of laughter. Seeing the change that had come over his wife, he decided to go back with her the next day. Now, standing there beside the pulpit telling this story, he was overcome by the power of the Spirit and fell out on the floor for the duration of the service.

A pastor from Jacksonville was introduced to share what God was doing in his life and church. He stepped to the pulpit and opened his mouth to speak, but no words came from his astonished lips. With a quizzical look on his face, he just stood there in silence. Several times he moved his head as if to speak, but no words came forth. He was literally struck dumb by the power of God. After what seemed like three or four minutes of attempting to speak, he finally pointed his left hand at the congregation, with his pointer finger extended and his thumb pointing upward like a cocked pistol. Suddenly, as rigid as a board, he fell backward to the floor, his finger now pointing at the ceiling and his thumb pointed toward the choir. He spent the rest of the service in that position. It was almost as though God was delighting in exposing the pridefulness of the human heart and showing us that He was not impressed with human dignity.

When Rodney Howard Browne finally got to preach, he did so above outbreaks of laughter all over the building. We found the laughter to be somewhat distracting, and to be honest, a bit annoying. It was difficult to concentrate on what Browne was saying because of the noise of the laughter. The final straw was when a husband/wife couple sitting on the pew in front of us was spontaneously and simultaneously smitten by this laughing phenomenon. I was tempted to leave at that point, but two things kept me in my seat. I was afraid that our leaving would be distracting, and secondly, I was afraid we would miss something.

When the evangelist began to pray for people, almost everyone he touched fell to the floor. Now, I had seen people "slain in the Spirit" before and that did not particularly impress me. I had even prayed for hundreds of people in my ministry who had fallen out on the floor under the power of God. The difference here was that almost everybody he prayed for fell on the floor. It was literally "wall-to-wall" people. The floor was so full that the crowd spilled out into the hallway surrounding the auditorium. The hallway floor was also filled with prostrate bodies. Time and space do not allow us here to elaborate on the lasting effects of that revival. History will have to judge what eternal ramifications came as a result of that series of meetings. My purpose is simply to show you the part this revival played in the Gainesville outpouring.

On the way home from the service, I was curious to know how my staff felt about the service we had just been in. I was careful not to voice my own opinion first, because I did not want to influence their honest opinion of what they had experienced. Amazingly, we discovered that all of us had come away with the same opinion. We did not particularly like all the demonstrations that we had seen, especially the laughter; yet, we could not escape the fact that we ALL felt that we had been in the presence of a supernatural God! A hunger was birthed in our hearts that night. Our prayer was, "Father, we don't want a revival that looks like that one; but, we do want a supernatural visitation of your Spirit!" Little did we know that you can't tell God how to do His business.

THE HUNGER GROWS:

A few weeks later, I came across a videotaped documentary of the Asbury revival of the 1970's. I decided to show it to our congregation on a Wednesday night. It details how God spontaneously moved in a morning chapel service in a Methodist college in Kentucky. The chapel service extended uninterrupted throughout the day into the night. Before the week was over, word had spread all across America of what was happening at Asbury. The following weekend, churches as far away as the west coast were hearing personal experiences of students who had flown home to share what God was doing. On the videotape, there were personal testimonies of people whose lives had been changed in that revival.

When the video came to an end, I stepped up to the microphone and asked our congregation for their comments and observations. For a moment, there was an awkward silence. Finally, someone asked, "Pastor, if God can do that in a Methodist college, why can't we have revival in a Pentecostal church?" The answer to that question was obvious; God will send revival to any people who are hungry enough and who will cry out to God for His intervention in their lives. The hunger in our hearts was growing more and more intense.

In my pridefulness, I had somehow always assumed that when God decided to send revival to Gainesville, He would naturally send it to the First Assembly of God and that I, as pastor, would play the primary role in that revival. How subject we pastors are to that horrible sin of pride, if only we would dare to admit it! But, my hunger for God was growing larger than my pride. I found myself praying, "Father, I don't care where you send revival in our city, or who the human leader of that revival is. I just want it to happen, and I want to be a part of it! At that point in time, I had no way of knowing what God had in store for us or how closely it was going to parallel that prayer.

THE CASE OF THE BACKWARD COLLAR

I don't know where it came from or when it began, but I've always had an intense dislike for clerical collars. In my opinion, they represented an air of superiority. I felt that people who wore them did so because they were prideful and arrogant about their station in life. In fact, I sure was proud that I didn't wear one of those horrid things! How ironic that God was about to smack me in the face with not one, but three of them.

Lou and Joan Mattia were co-rectors of Saint Michael's Episcopal Church in Gainesville and they were fellow members of the local ministerial association with me. With the excitement of two school children who had just found out that the circus was coming to town, Lou and Joan came in and began handing out flyers for an upcoming revival they were having at their church.

"We've never had a revival!" they laughingly said. "In fact, we've never even been in a revival; we don't even know what a revival is, but we're going to have one!"

I took one of their flyers and read the details of the meeting. My mouth fell open in amazement when I saw the name of Father Bud Williams of Lakeland, Florida. I did not know Bud personally, but I did know who he was. He had been one of the people who had been laid out on the floor in the Rodney Howard Browne revival a few months before!

"Are you sure you know what you're getting yourself in for?" I asked them. "You're church will never be the same again if you go through with this! This guy's not your run-of-the-mill Episcopalian. He'll have people lying out on the floor and your Episcopalian pews will rock with laughter. This is not the kind of stuff that Episcopalians are made of. You had better re-think this!"

"Arnold," Joan said, "They're already dead! How much damage can he do?" She had a point, and I had no answer. Then, I said something that surprised even me.

"Well, if there's anything I can do to help, just let me know." Little did I know what all that would involve.

A few days later, I got a call from Joan. "Arnold," she said, "Bud's office just called and they want us to have some drums for the service; could we borrow some drums and a drummer from you?" Thinking how generous I was, I said,

"Sure, I think we can help you with that."

"He said he wanted a worship team, too. We don't have one of those. Can you help us with that?" she said.

Knowing that my worship team would jump at the opportunity to sing to a new congregation, I gave her an affirmative answer. Not realizing the spot she was putting me in, Joan then asked,

"Could you get us some 'catchers'? He said we would need some catchers, also. I didn't have the heart to tell her that we didn't even have 'catchers' in our church, so I quietly agreed to get some for her, wondering whom I could tap for the job.

Congratulating myself for how magnanimous and ecumenical I was being, I even announced their upcoming revival services in our church. In fact, on the Sunday when their revival was scheduled to begin I even announced to our congregation, "Tonight, we will have services as usual at our church. However, if any of you really want to attend St. Michael's revival, I release you to go there with a clear conscience." "How generous of me," I thought.

That night, our usual crowd showed up for the service. In fact, it did not seem to be diminished at all. However, I sensed in my spirit that most of them were just there out of a sense of loyalty to their pastor and their church, and that, given the opportunity, most of them would be at St. Michael's church. So, I said to them,

"I really appreciate your coming tonight; but I really sense in my spirit that most of you would rather be at St. Michael's for the revival. If you would really rather be there…be honest…raise your hand."

Almost every hand in the church went up! "OK, OK, well, we're going to receive our offering and I'm going to let you go so you can get there in time for the opening of their service. I need to tell you however, that I am not in charge of the service and I am not responsible for anything you may see or experience at that meeting."

"If that's a disclaimer, Pastor, you're too late!" someone said from the audience.

"What are you talking about?" I asked.

"Obviously you didn't read yesterday's newspaper," she said. "There was a large advertisement for the revival that lists First Assembly of God as a cooperating church."

"You've got to be kidding!" I said. (She wasn't!) "Then, we had better get over there to look after our interests!" So, off we went to Saint Michael's Episcopal Church where our drummer, our worship team, and our catchers were already there.

MY CONFRONTATION WITH THE COLLAR

The building was quite full when we arrived, but we managed to find seats and my wife and I ended up down near the front. Bud Williams and his keyboard player, Gary, led the service almost entirely. It was obvious that they were experienced in this atmosphere and they were right at home. Gary was very adept at leading the people into worship and Bud seemed to be very responsive to the right time to minister to people's needs. I was, however, a bit disappointed in what I perceived to be an overemphasis on external manifestations such as falling out on the floor and "holy laughter."

My heart was torn in several directions. Part of me was feeling very protective of my people, not wanting them to be exposed to heresy or spiritual excesses. Another part of me was enjoying the opportunity to minister in song with the worship team during the altar services. But, most of all was my own deep hunger for God to do something supernatural in what I had come to call "my city." I wanted to be open to whatever God wanted to do, but I did not want to be responsible for leading my congregation into heresy.

Meanwhile, my son, Allen had called me from Lakeland to tell me that he felt that he had a "word from the Lord" for me. He told me that he felt that God wanted me not to miss a single service (morning and night) in Bud Williams' revival. I told Allen that I would make the effort, but inside I wasn't so sure that he had heard from God. As it turned out, I did not miss a single service that week.

Early in the week, Bud made a disturbing announcement. He said that on Friday morning he was going to have a "transfer of the anointing" service. He said that God had placed a special anointing on his life through the laying on of Rodney Howard Browne's hands, and that he was going to transfer that anointing to us pastors. I wasn't quite sure how I felt about that! In the first place, I wasn't sure I even believed in this "transfer of anointing" business. I didn't believe it could be supported in scripture. Secondly, I didn't think this young squirt of an Episcopalian had anything to transfer to me! If anybody ought to be laying on hands, I should be laying hands on him! Why, I've been saved more years than he has been born! He's practically a baby Christian, and he's gonna lay hands on me? Incredibly, through all of this, I never would have confessed to any pridefulness on my part.

Determined to prove him wrong, I went home and began to search the Bible for answers on the "transfer of anointing" thing. Much to my surprise, I found more than I had expected. I found how Samuel had anointed David in I Samuel 16:13 where the scripture said that "Samuel took the horn of oil, and anointed him in the midst of his brethren: and the Spirit of the LORD came upon David from that day forward." I remembered that God had told Elijah to "anoint Elisha to be prophet in thy room" and how Elisha took Elijah's mantle in 2 Kings 2 and the anointing of "prophet in Israel" passed to his shoulders that day. I remembered how the anointing as leader of Israel passed from Moses to Joshua and God promised to be with him just as He had been with Moses. Then, decisively, I remembered how Paul had instructed Timothy to "stir up the gift of God, which is in thee by the putting on of my hands." It is true that God was the acting Agent on every one of these occasions, but He chose to use men as instruments in the transfer process. My argument against the "transfer of anointing" was crumbling under the weight of scriptural evidence to the contrary.

Still, I was uncomfortable with the idea. It had not yet occurred to me that the real issue was my pride. I simply did not want a young Episcopalian priest with a "turned-around collar" laying hands on me and praying for me. So, I figured out how I could avoid the issue. When he called for those who wanted to be prayed for to come forward, I simply would not go. People would assume that I already had that anointing and that I didn't need to go forward. I would simply slip to the worship team while he prayed for the other pastors who really needed it! But, God was wise to me; He had another idea.

When Friday morning came, I went to the service thinking that I had figured out a solution to the dilemma. But, when the time for ministry came, my plan suddenly began to fall apart. He did not give an invitation; he gave a command! "Will all the pastors please come forward; I want to pray for you now." What to do, what to do? If I went forward, I would be admitting that I needed this young Episcopalian's prayer. If I did not go forward, it would look like I was in rebellion and it would make me look bad. God had figured out a way to use my own pride as a weapon against me! What a smart God!

Feeling that I had been outsmarted and that I had no other alternative; I ended up going forward with 20-30 other pastors who were in the service. We ended up standing with our toes against the semi-circular altar of the church, with Bud Williams standing on the other side of the altar rail. Bud is not a very loud or demonstrative man. He simply walked by and prayed for each of us. He would anoint the forehead with oil and then pray a simple prayer asking God to transfer a special anointing upon this pastor. Before he got to where I was standing I began to pray.

"Father, I didn't really want to be here, but apparently you want me here. At any rate, I am here. So, since I am here, why don't you do something really supernatural with me? Blow me away with your Presence, Lord. Lay me out on the floor and do a mighty work in me. Zap me, Lord! Come on; zap me! Now, Lord!"

I felt Bud's finger on my forehead, anointing me with oil, and I heard him softly praying, "Lord Jesus, let a holy anointing of your Presence come into Brother Arnold right now. Let this great anointing that you have placed in me, now be placed in him." And then he moved on to pray for someone else.

Is that it? What happened? No cold chills? No dazzling light? No laying out on the floor? Nothing! Nada! Zilch! Zip! Is this all there was to it? By now I was conscious that Bud had stopped praying for the pastors. I opened my eyes and looked around, and who was the only one left standing on his feet? Me! Now, I began to get a little annoyed.

"What's wrong with me, Lord? Why would you lay everybody else out, but not me? I thought You didn't play favorites. Why am I the only one standing? It isn't fair, God!"

The service ended and, disappointed, I took my wife, Joy and we headed to lunch. We hadn't even gotten out of the parking lot when she turned to me and said,

"Well, what happened, Honey?" I didn't want to hear that question because I didn't have a good answer.

"Nothing," I snapped, "Absolutely nothing. I didn't feel a thing!"

"Well, I thought it was a good service. I really felt the Lord's Presence," she said, apparently disappointed that I did not share her enthusiasm. Wives...sometimes they can be a real pain!

Somehow, I overcame my disappointment and made it back to the service that night for the closing night of the revival. The service was about like the other nights; but, this time, instead of praying for the people who came forward, Bud dropped a bombshell!

"Tonight, I'm not praying for anybody. These pastors who were prayed for this morning will be doing the praying. Pastors, please join us at the front."

Oh, no! I felt like I had been trapped. There was no way out. Now, people would be expecting us to be carbon copies of Bud Williams, and that just wasn't me. Again, God used my pride against me. If I did not go forward to pray for people it would make me look bad. And, so I went, albeit very reluctantly.

To make matters worse, Bud had a layman accompanying him in his revivals. He called him his "administrator" and part of his job was to organize the altar services to minimize the confusion of a large response. He did his job well, but from my perspective his style tended to be somewhat abusive. I called him "Mr. Finger Snapper." When he wanted you to do something, he would snap his fingers and then bark an order at you. I complied, but believe me it wasn't joyfully.

The altar response was quite large that night—far too large for us to minister to them at the altar. Mr. Finger Snapper had a better idea. He herded us all out the back door of the church across the breezeway into the church vestry hall (fellowship hall.) He had already placed lines of tape on the carpet about 6 feet apart. He instructed the people to line up side by side with their toes on the tape. In retrospect, it all made sense. When people would fall out under the power of God they would not fall on each other; there was six feet of space for them. Pretty smart! But, at the time it all seemed so mechanical to me.

My attitude was rotten. I didn't want to be there. There was no music, no spiritual ambience, nothing. "God, you're a million miles away from this place!" I complained. "How did you get me into this mess?"

My grumbling was interrupted by the "snap, snap" of Mr. Finger Snapper's fingers. "Pastor Arnold, please move to the beginning of that first row and don't begin praying for people until I tell you to do so." I didn't know whether to salute or to say "Heil, Hitler!"

Finally, everybody was in the room, standing with their toes on the line and the word came down for us to begin praying for the people. Obediently, but reluctantly, I raised my hands to begin praying for the man in front of me.

I would be less than honest if I did not tell you that something supernatural happened at that precise moment. I felt a mantle of power come upon me as I began to raise my hands. I was conscious of God's mighty power present in the room. I lifted my hands to the level of the man's face and simply whispered, "In the name of Jesus…" My voice trailed off as the man fell to the floor weeping under the power of God. I had never even touched Him! Amazed, I went to the next person and experienced the same results. And, then, another. Finally, I came to a man who seemed to be totally unaffected by my prayer. I laid hands on him and I expected to see him fall to the floor; but he did not. I backed away and looked at my hands. "Easy come; easy go!" I thought. "Where did you go, Lord? Don't leave me now!"

And, then I heard His still, small voice speak to my spirit, "I haven't gone anywhere, son; I'm still here. Remember this morning when Bud Williams prayed for you? Did you fall to the floor? Yet, do you doubt now that I did something in you this morning? I don't always have to lay a person out on the floor to accomplish what I want to do in them. It wasn't necessary for me to lay you out on the floor this morning to do what I wanted to do."

Now, it all made sense to me. The whole week seemed to fall into place for me. Then, God spoke again, "Now tell this man standing before you what I just told you."

I shared my experience with the man and told him that God didn't have to lay him out on the floor to do what needed to be done. He seemed so relieved to hear that word. Ironically, when I prayed for him again, he did fall to the floor under the power of God. Before the night was over, I had opportunity to use that message several times as I prayed for others in the line.

NOW IT'S OUR TIME

As the meeting at St. Michael's came to a close, a small delegation of people from my church came to me to ask if we could have Bud Williams come to preach a revival at the First Assembly of God. Their request confirmed what I was already feeling in my spirit. I approached Bud about the possibility. Unfortunately, the only time he had open was in the middle of the summer—not a good time in the church calendar. Nevertheless, I took it and I scheduled Bud to be with us for ten days in July.

Not all of our people had attended St. Michael's revival in the spring. The time leading up to July gave me time to prepare their hearts for what God would be doing. I had the opportunity to preach a series of messages on revival. I was able to plow up the ground, plant the seed, and get ready for the harvest that God was going to bring. By the time Bud came to be with us, we were ready.

Despite the fact that it was the middle of the summer, it proved to be the best revival we have ever had. Our building seats about 400 packed. We averaged 454 per night, with chairs down the aisles. On Sunday night, we packed in over 550 people! Many lives were impacted and changed during that time period, including mine.

I confess to you that the one thing I had the greatest problem with was the "holy laughter" phenomenon. I believed that God could manifest Himself that way if He chose to, but I still had a problem with it. I guess the best word I can use for my feelings is "tolerance." I could tolerate people "laughing in the Spirit" but I didn't particularly like it. Unknown to me, God had a "housetop experience" for me.

One night after the revival services had come to an end, I was preaching an intense message on "Forgiveness and the Infilling of the Holy Spirit." I was emphasizing that we often ask God to fill us with His Spirit, but we have so much unforgiveness and other junk inside of us that there's no room for the Spirit to dwell. I was encouraging the congregation to let God empty you before He fills you. Suddenly, from deep inside my being, I felt a chuckle come up my throat and out of my mouth.

"What was that, God?" I thought. "I don't have time for this; I'm right in the middle of something serious here; I'm trying to make a point and You're interrupting a great sermon, God!!"

Just then, I felt another rumble of laughter come up my throat and escape my lips. In a matter of seconds I was convulsing with laughter. I was a mixed bag of feelings. On the one hand, I was very embarrassed to be doing this in full view of my congregation. On the other hand, it felt so good that I didn't want it to stop. I staggered over to the wall and leaned against it until I could regain control of myself. When I managed to do so, I saw that my congregation was consumed with laughter too. However, I'm not so sure theirs was "holy laughter." I think they were just amused to see God humble their starchy pastor. My feelings about the laughter phenomenon were forever changed after that personal experience.

Fourteen years have passed since that revival encounter in Gainesville. The long-term effects on the church have been astounding. The church has quadrupled in size, built a new building, and lives have been changed. The spirit of unity in the church has been remarkable. And, it all began when the people of God got hungry. It is still true that "If my people, which are called by my name, shall humble themselves, and pray, and seek my face, and turn from their wicked ways; then will I hear from heaven, and will forgive their sin, and will heal their land." (2 Chronicles 7:14 KJV)

Chapter Ten

The Haiti Years

From the time of my first call to ministry in my teenage years, I had somehow felt that one day I would be a missionary to Haiti. I thought that I would probably spend my life preaching to the Haitians in French. I even studied the French language for five years in order to be able to do exactly that. At the time I did not even realize that Creole was the native language of Haiti, not French. In the wisdom and providence of God, He never saw fit to send me to Haiti as a resident missionary. He did, however, allow me to visit the country frequently and to be involved in several missionary ventures there. We have been privileged to build a church building in St. Marc, an orphanage in Port au Prince and to make over a dozen medical and construction trips to this impoverished nation. Some of the greatest miracles I have ever witnessed took place in Haiti.

OUR FIRST TRIP TO HAITI

The flight from Miami to Port au Prince had been uneventful for our ragtag band of medical missionaries. Among others, our team included a pastor, an automobile mechanic, an insulation installer, a few college students and missionary Miriam Fredericks. Our most knowledgeable medical personnel were Miriam (a Registered Nurse specializing in jungle medicine), my wife, Joy (a Licensed Practical Nurse) and a couple of nursing students.

If the flight had been uneventful, the trip to Petit-tous-de-Nips was anything but that. We were met at the airport by a ramshackle truck garishly painted with every color of the rainbow and religious sayings in French to keep the evil spirits away. The back of the truck had been covered to keep out the rain and horizontal railings placed along the sides to let in some air. Unpadded wooden benches had been installed for passengers to sit in. We found out that these vehicles were Haiti's answer to mass transit and are called "Tap-taps." They got their name from the practice of tapping on the roof when you get to the place where you want to get off. The driver usually has an assistant at the rear of the truck that collects your fare as you unceremoniously depart from the back of the truck.

In our case the tap-tap had been rented for our use alone so we threw our luggage on and climbed aboard. We were eager to get the vehicle moving so we could get some relief from the broiling tropical sun. None too soon, we were on our way for what Gilligan would have called "a three-hour tour…a three-hour tour." Seven hours later we arrived at Petit-tous-de-Nips. Darkness had overtaken us and we had to load our luggage and supplies into the little boats by flashlight. With more trust than was warranted, we committed ourselves to the care of the Haitian drivers of the boats. With nothing more than their instincts and experience to guide them they ferried us around the peninsula to the little village of Zetoit, accessible only by boat and foot trails.

There was no electricity in Zetoit and the only way we knew we had arrived was the sound of voices on the shore. Our boatmen nosed our boats onto the shore and using our flashlights we stepped gingerly into the mud, carrying our suitcases with us. Very quickly we felt unseen hands pulling our suitcases away from us. This was no small source of concern, since we had been warned to hold tightly to our luggage at the airport or you may never see it again. Fortunately, such was not the case in Zetoit; these hands were helpful hands wanting only to honor their guests who had come so far to help them.

Joy and I pitched our little tent by flashlight. Then, we blew up our air mattresses, made our beds and settled in for the night. The last thing I remember was the sounds of Voodoo drums and hundreds of whispering voices of people who had walked for miles from all over the jungle. They had no promise of anything; only the hope that someone would be able to provide some help for the many diseases that plagued them.

A NEW DAY DAWNS

I had heard that demons were widely found in Haiti but I had never associated anything demonic with roosters…not until that night, anyway. Somewhere between midnight and dawn they began to sound off. I concluded that they were either demon possessed or else roosters in Haiti couldn't tell time very well. At any rate, by the time the sun rose I was already awake. I pushed the tent flap aside and thrust my head out into the morning light. I was surprised to see the inquisitive faces of scores of children who were curious to know more about the white-skinned Americans who had come to visit them. Obvious signs of malnutrition and disease were commonplace among them, and I couldn't help but wonder if they ever really experienced the normal joys of childhood. The day had just begun and my heart was aching already.

I opened a loaf of bread to make some breakfast, only to find that the rats had beaten me to the bread. With disgust I threw the contaminated bread over the fence. Why I should have been surprised I do not know, but to my amazement the children went scrambling after the discarded loaf of bread. I guessed that contaminated bread was better than no bread at all. From that moment on, nothing went to waste in our camp.

THE DOCTOR IS IN

My knowledge of medicine consists of being able to read the label on a bottle of aspirins (provided the type is not too small.) However, I have always felt that organization is one of my strengths. I asked Miriam what needed to be done and then I went about the business of getting it done. We cleared out the benches in the tiny little church in the jungle and began to set up our makeshift clinic. Outside on the ground, we set up the "wash and lube" department. It was here that we took the babies and thoroughly washed them in soap and water. We then slathered them with a concoction of Vaseline and sulfur to serve as a soothing emollient to the suffering children. At one door, we set up an Intake Center. Their job was to evaluate the patients and try to determine what kind of care they needed. They would then route them to whatever area of the room they needed to be in. In one corner of the room we stationed a former medical corpsman in the Army. His job was to attend to open wounds. In another corner of the little chapel/clinic we set up an inoculation area where shots were given for many different kinds of problems.

In yet another corner of the room there was our answer to the ENT (ear, nose, and throat) center.

Finally, at the exit door to the building we placed our pharmacy table. It was here that we dispensed what little medicine that we had at our disposal. Because of her experience as a nurse who dispensed medications, my wife, Joy headed up our pharmacy.

In the middle of this mass of disorganized chaos of over 600 people begging for help, I began to utilize my organizational skills. I assigned various personnel to different workstations, herded all of the prospective patients outside the building and began to bring some order to all the confusion. Our crowd control guys were only allowing a certain number of patients into the building at a time. Miriam (our RN missionary) had taught me how to take blood pressures and I was assisting the intake personnel in determining where the patients needed to be directed.

Barking orders, with a stethoscope hung around my neck, I must have looked every bit the part of a jungle doctor. Heavily engrossed in what I was doing, I almost didn't notice the reluctant tap on my shoulder. I turned and looked down into the tearful face of a tiny Haitian mother who was holding her baby out to me and speaking something in Creole. I had no idea of what she was saying, but I assumed that she wanted me to look at her baby and decide what kind of treatment he needed. Just as I reached out to take the child, I heard Miriam yell at me above the noise of the clinic.

"No, no, Pastor; don't take that child!" she said. Sensing the alarm in Miriam's voice and wondering what kind of terrible communicable disease the child must have, I drew back from the woman and her child and turned toward where Miriam was standing.

"Why not?" I asked, puzzled by the sound of alarm in Miriam's voice.

"Because, she wants to give you her baby!" she responded.

"Of course, I know that," I protested, a little annoyed at Miriam's interference.

"No, I mean she wants to GIVE you her baby!" she said, with a strong emphasis on the word "give." "That will be YOUR baby if you take him."

"But, why would she want to give me her baby?" I asked.

"Because, she knows he's dying and she can't help him. She thinks that if he is yours, you will save him. She would rather give him up than to see him die."

I looked into the pleading face of that little mother and suddenly every ounce of emotion in my body came surging to my face. I knew I was going to lose it, and I started looking for a place to hide my anguish. The only thing available was an old, two-compartment orange crate that the church used as a pulpit. I fell to my knees, buried my face in the orange crate so no one could see my tears and wept profusely.

I felt so useless. My years of theological training had not prepared me for this. This was human need in the raw and I wasn't ready for it. Who was I kidding? I'm no doctor!

"Why would you bring me here, God? I don't have the training it takes; I'm no good to anybody here. Why me, God?" I took out my frustration and futility on God.

I believe God spoke to me in that Haitian jungle, with my head in an old orange crate. "One thing is certain, son; you're no good to anybody with your head buried in a box. Now, get up and do what you can." Those words have become my mantra for every mission trip since then; "Now, get up and do what you can!"

HISLAIRE JEAN

When the day was finished and we had no more strength to give, we had seen less than half the sick people who had come for help. We literally wept as over 300 people went back into the jungle, having received no help from us at all. It was a small consolation that 300 people were helped because we were there.

One of those who were helped was a frail little 6-year old boy suffering from "dry" malnutrition. (In "wet" malnutrition the child becomes bloated, retaining fluid and often dies of congestive heart failure. In "dry" malnutrition the flesh wastes away until the bony skeleton shows through the skin.)

Hislaire Jean was so undernourished that he was curled into a straw basket on top of his mother's head. She could not have weighed more than a hundred pounds and stood less than 5 feet tall. It was obvious to us that Hislaire Jean was dying. If he had any chance at all, we had to get him to a hospital in Port au Prince. The "tap-tap" bus would not be back for us for two days. Meanwhile we were faced with the daunting task of keeping him alive. Our answer to that was peanut butter sandwiches and Gatorade.

Hislaire Jean may have been in a weakened physical state, lying there in his mother's basket, but his spirit was indomitable. He refused everything we offered him to eat, and informed us in Creole that he would eat nothing but rice and beans that his "Mama" had prepared for him. Feeling up to his challenge, I took a piece of Haitian bread, smeared a generous coating of peanut butter on it and tried to place it in his mouth. Rebelliously, he turned his face away and protested my efforts. With more than a little "not-so-righteous indignation" I determined that no 6-year old kid could out-stubborn me! I held his head and jammed the peanut butter and bread into his protesting mouth. For a moment he angrily spit and sputtered peanut butter and bread everywhere. But then, he licked his mouth and got his first taste of peanut butter. His eyes grew wide, his cries grew silent, and his little bony hand grabbed the peanut butter and bread from my hand. Soon, he was filling that little belly with piece after piece of peanut buttered bread and Gatorade. In a little while, he fell asleep in his mother's arms for what we all believed to be their last night together.

The next morning we gathered our gear together and boarded the leaky boats that were to take us to the next village. The little mother stood on the shore crying, holding Hislaire Jean in her arms. Just before we pushed away from the shore, she handed him to us in the boat. Mother and baby were both crying. As we moved away from the shore, Hislaire Jean suddenly stopped crying and started singing a mournful tune. Miriam's eyes were filled with tears as she instructed the boatman to take us back to the shore.

"I can't stand this," she said, "He's made up a song in Creole and he's singing it to his mother! He's telling how the white people have come and taken him away from his mother and he will never see his mother again." We left Hislaire Jean in his mother's arms.

But, not for long. The teenagers of our team had taken the arduous trip up the mountain to hold clinic in an even more remote region. Our 14-year old son, Jon was among that group. They were to follow along behind us the next day. Miriam had left the "dirty work" up to them. They were to bring Hislaire Jean with them the next day.

Jon had not wanted to come to Haiti in the first place. He was going through the "disease" known as "fourteen." (Any parent who has ever had a fourteen year-old will understand that.) As it turned out, it was there that Jon received his call to ministry.

For some unexplained reason, Jon and Hislaire Jean bonded with each other. In fact, they were literally inseparable. Peanut butter therapy had done wonders for Hislaire Jean and he was now able to walk and respond to people. His strong will became even more apparent with each passing day.

When we finally arrived in Port au Prince, we checked into the hotel for a day of rest and relaxation. At the check-in desk, the clerk heard Hislaire Jean asking for some black beans and rice. He captured her heart and she went into her kitchen and cooked him some before we took him to his room.

Jon and Hislaire Jean shared the same hotel room. Jon undressed Hislaire Jean and was about to take him for a shower. It was obvious that modesty was not a problem to him; no doubt there were many days when he wore no clothes at all. What none of us expected was his reaction to the full-length mirror on the wall. It never occurred to us that he had never seen himself in a mirror. His first reaction was shocked curiosity at who the people were in the room that looked exactly like us! He raised his hand and watched in amazement as the little boy in the mirror also raised his hand. Then, he wiggled his fingers and watched the other little boy do the same. He grinned, and his little black lips framed those white teeth in the biggest grin you could possibly imagine. A star was born!

We checked Hislaire Jean into the hospital, knowing that upon his release he would be placed in our orphanage in Port au Prince. Our church agreed to pay the cost of Hislaire Jean's stay at the orphanage and his education. With those arrangements made, we boarded our plane and flew back to the States, with a sense of satisfaction in a job well done.

Because the orphanage directors were missionaries from our church (Terry & Vickie Butler) we received frequent updates on Hislaire Jean. But, I don't think any of us were quite prepared for what we saw when we returned a year later. Although the orphanage accepted children up to age 12, because of his strong will and innate leadership qualities, six-year-old Hislaire Jean had evolved into the "leader of the pack." All the other kids, even the older ones, looked to Hislaire Jean for leadership. And, his leadership was all good.

Despite his initial objections to Christianity (he protested that he did not need Jesus because he had the demon spirits to guide him), he soon accepted Jesus as his Savior. Even at the tender age of six, his spiritual growth was amazing.

Hislaire was strong and healthy again and Terry was trying to place him into an adoptive home in Florida. Haitian law, however, requires parental consent in order for that to happen. Knowing that the parents could not afford to raise him, Terry sent for them to come to Port au Prince to sign the necessary paper work. They agreed. However, upon arriving and seeing how healthy he was, they refused to sign the papers.

"What do you want me to do with him, then?" Terry asked.

"Keep him until he is twelve, and we will come get him." they responded.

"No way!" Terry responded. "I know what you want! You just want someone to support you. You don't really love this child. I will never agree to that!"

Terry tried a bluff. "Either you sign these papers right now, or you take him with you today! I will not keep him five more years to turn him into a breadwinner for you!" Terry's bluff failed; they decided to take Hislaire Jean home with them. "I warn you," Terry said, "I will come to Zetoit from time to time, and if I find Hislaire in the condition he was before, I will take you to court and seek custody of him, even without your consent!" Undeterred by Terry's threat, and much to his chagrin, the parents took Hislaire Jean and trekked off into the jungle.

True to his word, the following year, Terry made a trip to Zetoit and made a special visit to the jungle hut of Hislaire Jean's family. In that year, the little seven-year old boy had led his entire family to Jesus and they were all attending the little church where we first met him! He had become a 7-year old evangelist in the remote jungle of Haiti!

HEAD TO HEAD WITH VOODOO MAGIC

Out team of 18 adults was still bone-tired from a grueling day of clinic in Hislaire Jean's home village of Zetoit on the north shore of the boot-shaped country that is Haiti. We arrived by boat at the little coastal village of Pestel, built right out over the water. We had no activities scheduled until that evening when we would conduct an evangelistic service in the village church. So, we spent our time walking through the village and visiting the open-air market. It was amusing to watch the little children, many of whom had never seen a white person. Their eyes wide with amazement, they would cautiously slip up beside us and rub the skin on our hands. "Blanc," they would say, "Blanc." They were trying to see if the white would rub off our skin. We must have looked like walking ghosts to them.

We enjoyed our leisure time, but we were fully ready when service time came that night. People turned out from throughout the jungle surrounding Pestel. The little church was full and overflowing and the results in the altar call were gratifying.

On a sad note, we lost our battle for one baby's life during the night. We had taken eight malnourished babies from the jungle on that trip. Only four survived the trip. This particular child suffered from "wet" malnutrition. In this form of the disease, the body retains fluid and becomes bloated. The surface tissues of the body begin to break down and lesions often appear. Fluid begins to build up inside the body and the heart finds it difficult to beat (a condition known as "congestive heart failure.") Death soon follows. Miriam, Joy, and Walt (our military corpsman) took turns administering CPR to keep the baby alive. After hours of futile efforts, they finally had to give up and the little life ended. Ironically, an inexpensive diuretic tablet called Lasix might well have saved his life—a tablet that we did not have.

The next morning we awakened, expecting to meet the truck that was to pick us up and take us back to Port au Prince. One thing we learned early in our trips to Haiti was flexibility. Things seldom go the way you plan; you always have to have an alternate plan. As the day wore on, it became increasingly clear that the truck was not going to arrive in time to get us back to the capitol.

About 5:30 in the afternoon, Miriam convened everyone together to discuss our options. We had already held a service in Pestel the night before and we did not want to hold another one two nights in a row. She told us of a village about an hour and a half away by boat. She said that she did not usually take groups there because it was such a hotbed of Voodoo worship. However, since we were all mature adults, she would take us to Corail if we wanted to go there. It sounded like a challenging adventure, so with a unanimous show of hands we all voted to go to Corail.

After hastily gathering enough gear to keep us overnight, eighteen adults crowded into a little 17 ft. wooden boat with a six horsepower, kerosene-powered outboard motor known as a "kicker." The first person into the boat picked up a can and began to bail water from the boat. We did not stop bailing until we reached our destination. Despite our best efforts, we barely kept up with the leaking water coming into the boat.

At first, there was an air of celebration and singing in the boat. However, as the sun began sinking over the horizon and the shoreline became more and more difficult to see, our thoughts shifted toward the coral reefs lurking just below the surface of the water. As far as we knew, we were in great peril in the open water in a leaking boat with a 6-hp kerosene engine. Fortunately, our boatman had traveled these waters many times before. Between him and God, we were in good hands. But, we were praying and bailing nonetheless!

After about an hour and a half, we pulled alongside a long concrete wharf that had been erected by "Papa Doc" (the Haitian dictator) in order to curry the support of the people of Corail. They lived in poverty, but at least they had a dock.

It was so dark that we could see nothing. However, we could hear the sounds of what sounded like a large crowd of people. Miriam shined her light into the crowd until the beam fell upon the face of the pastor of the local church.

"Pastor, what are these people doing here?" she asked.

"We have come to welcome you." he responded.

"But, how did you know we were coming?" she pressed.

"We heard through the jungle drums that you were in Pestel last night. So, we met this morning at our church and 35 people fasted and prayed that God would bring you to Corail tonight. God told us you would come and we have come to welcome you."

We could hardly believe what we were hearing. 1½ hours earlier, we did not even know there was a place called Corail. Now, by the providence of God, we were there! What did God have up His sleeve? In the distance we could hear the guitars and drums already playing. They had already started church in anticipation of our arrival.

The little church was packed with people when we arrived. I knew that the logistics of the moment were so incredible that people would not believe it back home in the States. The next morning, I actually measured the building. It was 22 feet wide by 34 feet long, less than 750 square feet of space. By actual count, there were over 350 people in the building in the service that night!

When we entered the building, we literally elbowed our way through the crowd to get to the front of the church. In order to preach, I had to stand with my back in one corner of the building. Standing only inches from my face was a horrendous looking man with angry eyes. As I attempted to preach, he held his hand in the shape of a cobra coiled to strike and hissed at me. He would thrust his finger/fangs at me and hiss while I preached the Word. I was so angry with him that I wanted to take him outside and either cast the devil out of him or beat the devil out of him and I wasn't sure which I preferred! I couldn't understand why one of the local pastors did not do something about him. I was just the visiting preacher and I did not feel that it was my place to delve into local matters.

As I finished my message and began to give the altar call, the man turned to the congregation and began to hiss menacingly at them, daring them to come forward. In that congregation of 350 people, not one person came forward for prayer or ministry. Disappointed, I turned the service to the missionary and I slipped, unnoticed, out the rear door of the church.

After the service, my colleagues and I debriefed on the events of the evening. Why would God have orchestrated such a remarkable miracle to get to us to Corail, only to have us suffer such a shameful defeat at the hands of Satan? The only conclusion that we could reach was that God had something else in store for us the next day. With that in mind we bedded down for the night.

Thursday morning the roosters awakened us before day. After a light breakfast, our crew decided to head to the church and have another service. Where else but in Haiti would you call an impromptu service on Thursday morning and expect anyone to attend? But, the Haitians surprised us again. They had anticipated that we would have a service and when we arrived at the church they were already gathering. The musical instruments began playing and soon the church was full again.

I had purposed that I would not surrender to demonic forces again. If we could not rely on the local pastors to deal with the demoniacs, then we would do it ourselves. I delegated several of my colleagues to handle any manifestations that occurred during the service. This time, several teenage girls displayed similar hissing manifestations like the ones we had seen the night before. I would stop preaching only long enough to send workers to take them outside and cast the devils out of them. None of them proved to be any match for the power of God!

The Lord directed me to deal with the issue of unity in the church and recognizing the pastoral authority in the local church. It was "just what the doctor ordered" and there was a lot of weeping and hugging at the altar as people confessed their bad attitudes to each other. God did a wonderful healing in that service.

After the service was over we started gathering everyone together to board our boat back to Pestel. However, I was still smoldering from the Wednesday night service when the "snake man" had unrestricted access to our service and stopped us dead in the water. I wanted to reprimand somebody, but I didn't know who. I asked Miriam to gather all the local pastors together for a meeting. Six jungle pastors were there and we met under the banana trees behind the church. I rejoiced with them at the victories that were won in the morning service, but reprimanded them that no one had stepped forward to deal with the hissing man the night before. They looked at each other and then looked at me with questioning eyes. I was not prepared for their response to my angry rebuke.

"What should we have done, Pastor?" one of them said, apologetically.

Only then did I realize that they did not know how to deal with demonic forces. They were simple men of God who had gotten saved and just wanted to lead other people to Jesus. No one had ever trained them in how to be pastors. They knew nothing about spiritual authority or demon warfare. They knew much about Satan's tactics, but they knew nothing about how to deal with him. I had assumed that any pastor living under constant exposure to demon power would know how to deal with it. Wrong!

For the next two hours I taught them about spiritual authority and their roles as pastors. They sat there like little birds with open mouths taking in every word I spoke as if their lives depended upon it. I spoke as rapidly as I could so as to cover as much ground as possible in the time we had left. Miriam kept pointing to her watch to let me know that our time was running short and we had to get back to Pestel.

"Please don't leave us, Pastor!" they begged. "Stay with us for two weeks and we will get a hundred jungle pastors here for you to teach."

"I cannot stay; I have commitments in America." I protested. "But, I will come back and teach a Pastor's School."

Miriam sprang to her feet. "Don't tell them that, Pastor! So many people have promised to come and then we never hear from them again. I don't want them to be disappointed again."

Jim Carney, one of my deacons, was seated beside me. I turned to him for reassurance. "I don't see how we can NOT come, Pastor. These people need us."

"Tell them we will come back, Miriam…and WE WILL!"

True to our word, a few months later we returned to western Haiti with a television crew. For three days, hour after hour we taught them how to be pastors. We covered everything from modeling family life for the congregation, to sermon preparation, to dealing with demonic forces. We left the tapes and equipment with them so they could teach others in the months ahead. Our Haitian pastors failed to live up to their promise of 100 native pastors; but, they did come up with 55 dedicated men of God who went back to their congregations better equipped for the task God had called them to. Finally, we realized why God had orchestrated the Corail miracle service.

A MEDICAL BAG FOUND, A MIRACLE BIRTH AND A BABY RAISED FROM THE DEAD!

"I want to go to Haiti with you!" said the voice in the telephone. I had never met the man and had no idea what he was like. All I knew was that he was a medical doctor and that he professed to be a Roman Catholic. Haiti can be a spiritually challenging place and we had never knowingly allowed a non-believer to go with us on any of our missionary trips there. Certainly there are Catholics who are born-again believers, but many of them are Catholic in name only and I wasn't sure of this man's relationship with God.

"Come by my office and let's talk about it; there are some things I need to tell you." I said. We set up a mutually agreeable time and I hung up the phone. I purposed to find out as much as I could about this man before agreeing for him to come on the trip.

His appointment time came and I found out that he was a surgeon who discovered that he did not like the practice of medicine. He gave up his practice to return to the University of Florida to become a psychiatrist. His parents had lived in Haiti during the twenty years of his childhood. He was very familiar with the Haitian culture and spoke Creole fluently. This was too good to be true. We are planning a medical mission to Haiti and I have a surgeon who knows the Haitian people and fluently speaks their language! He's got everything going for him; but it has become apparent to me that he does not have a personal relationship with Jesus. What should I do?

"Carl, there's something you should know about us," I said; "We are Pentecostals. We sing with gusto, we pray with intensity, we worship loudly, we talk in tongues, we pray for miracles of healing, and sometimes we even dance in worship! Some folks would call us downright weird! Do you think you could handle that?"

Dr. Carl looked at me and said, "Pastor, I lived in Haiti for twenty years, I think I can handle that." Not quite sure that he could, I reluctantly said yes. I'm sure that my decision was swayed by the fact that I had such a valuable resource in one package in the person of Dr. Carl Butterfield.

Despite my misgivings, Dr. Carl fit right in with our group of temporary missionaries. Auto mechanics, carpenters, secretaries, students, lab technicians, various kinds of nurses, and now a medical doctor as well. Except for a few of us, most of us were ill-suited to staff the medical clinic we intended to provide in the mountains of La Gonave, an island in the Caribbean off the coast of Port au Prince, Haiti. But, here we were; and somehow we would manage to do what we believed God had called us to do.

Clearing customs in Port au Prince is always a challenge under the best of circumstances. We Americans frown on extortion in any form but a few trips through customs in Haiti causes you to appreciate how a well-placed $20 bill can facilitate your passage through the line. Many of our team were first-timers and their anticipation was already high. The added excitement at the airport had their adrenaline running at fever pitch. We boarded the "tap-taps" (garishly painted covered pick-up trucks used for public transportation) for the trip to the hotel. We settled in for a good night's sleep before boarding the boat for La Gonave early the next morning.

A Haitian ferryboat defies description. At best it is a leaking, rickety, wooden boat that is frequently overloaded with people, pigs, chickens or anything else that can be hauled for a profit. On this particular day American missionaries comprised most of the cargo. After an hour or two of sailing we arrived in the tiny coastal village of Zetoit (same name—different village from the one previously mentioned) on the north shore of La Gonave in the Bay of Port au Prince. There were not enough donkeys for everybody so the women rode while the chivalrous men walked or led the donkeys up the mountain trail to the little village, which was eagerly awaiting our arrival.

We were not prepared for what we found when we reached the top of the mountain. Over 300 people with various kinds and degrees of sickness were waiting for us. There was no time for rest. We

A Funny Thing Happened on the Way to the Pulpit

unpacked our medicines and quickly arranged the small church building as a makeshift clinic. On our arrival we had met a young 20-year old pregnant woman who had been in labor for two full days! Her husband's face was filled with fear; he feared that he was going to lose his young wife. He begged us to do something.

We strung some bed sheets in one corner of the chapel to form a primitive delivery room and dragged a wooden table in to be used as a delivery table. Meanwhile, Dr. Carl began searching for his medical bag with all his tools. He had borrowed over $5,000 worth of surgical tools from Shands Teaching Hospital at the University of Florida in Gainesville. For safekeeping, he had placed his Rolex watch in the bag as well. Poverty is so prevalent in Haiti and theft is such a way of life that your watch can be stolen right off your wrist!

Panic was etched into Carl's face as he reported to me that he could not find his medical bag with all his tools. We turned the camp upside down but with no success; the bag was nowhere to be found. All we could figure was that the bag had been lost or stolen from the "tap-tap" bus on the way to the boat dock that morning. As the trip organizer I am supposed to be the problem-solver. Desperately I had to face the fact that I could not solve this problem; I had no idea where the bag might be, or how we could utilize Dr. Carl's valuable skills on this trip. If only I had realized that the Real Problem Solver was in control of the situation and was about to show what He could do!

Just when I thought things could not get any worse, Dr. Carl dropped a bombshell on all of us. He had performed a pelvic exam on the young woman and reported that it would be impossible for her to give birth except with a C-section. The two pubic bones that normally separate to form the birth canal were fused together in a congenital deformity making it impossible for her to give birth naturally. Dr. Carl was an experienced surgeon and a C-section would have been a routine procedure for him except that all his tools were in the lost medical bag.

Then Carl hit us with the worst news of all; the baby's skull had been crushed in the protracted labor and the baby was already dead! There were no signs of life and the baby's skull had been crushed "like a bag of marbles." With the right equipment he could save the mother, but it was too late for the baby; this little girl's eyes would never open to the Haitian sunlight.

Still trying to do everything we knew how to do, we sent a runner down the mountain to the dilapidated clinic at Zetoit, hoping to get someone to come or to send us the needed instruments for the surgery. Not finding the clinic open, the runner never bothered to return to our temporary facility. Death is such a constant companion in the Haitian culture, that there is little concern for human life. In his mind, she was a dead woman and not worth the effort it would take for him to climb back up the mountain trail. The day wore on and the young woman's condition grew more and more serious as her energy resources began to wane.

"She's not going to make it unless we do something soon!" Carl said. I thought for a moment, and then reluctantly said,

"I've been hesitant to mention it, Carl, but I've got a pocket knife if you'd like to use it."

"Get it ready, Pastor, and I'll go check on how she's doing." He disappeared behind the bed sheet curtains and I began to sharpen my knife.

Behind the curtains, Dr. Carl was preparing his handpicked team of nurses for what he was about to do. Sensing the seriousness of the situation and the danger to the young woman's life, the team formed a circle around the delivery table and began to pray for the young woman. Being Pentecostal, several of them began to pray in the Holy Spirit, speaking in their prayer languages, praying earnestly for God to do something! It didn't seem to bother Dr. Carl; he was busy doing one final pelvic exam so he would know what to expect when he did the C-section.

It would be hard to describe the look on Dr. Carl's face when he came out from behind the curtain. Puzzlement is the best word I can come up with.

"What's the situation, Carl?" I asked.

"I think we're going to have a baby!" he replied.

"I know that, Carl! I mean, what are we going to do?" I asked in exasperation.

"No, you don't understand," he said, "She's going to give birth naturally!"

"But, I thought you said…" My voice trailed off.

"I did, and she can't, but she is! I'll explain later!" And, he disappeared behind the curtain.

In a few minutes a cheer went up from behind the makeshift delivery room curtains. The young woman's fused pubic bones had miraculously separated and formed a birth canal and she had given birth to a stillborn little girl. After the initial euphoria the delivery room team grew sadly silent as they realized that the baby was lifeless, just as Dr. Carl had predicted.

Carl held the lifeless baby in his hands, frustrated at not having been able to do anything for the child. But, even now, doing nothing was not an option. Hurriedly, he began to clear the child's mouth and throat and to administer CPR to the lifeless infant. The delivery room team went into action again, praying fervently for the child's life. After what seemed like an eternity (estimated to have been 4-5 minutes) the child suddenly coughed, took a deep breath and began to cry! The whole building exploded in shouts of praise! The birth of this child had become everybody's primary project.

After cleaning up the child, examining her and pronouncing her healthy, strong, and normal in every way, Dr. Carl retired for a little rest and some serious thinking about what had happened.

The young Haitian father was so overcome with gratitude to have his wife and child safe and sound that he insisted that we pick a name for his daughter. After discussing it among ourselves, we decided that her name should be Rachel—and so it was! After resting for a few hours, the young father and his exhausted wife took their new baby and walked many miles home through the jungle. Such is life in the primitive regions of Haiti.

It was customary that we hold night services wherever we conducted medical clinics. This time was no different. The makeshift clinic was converted back into a church for those who had stayed for services that night. I preached a simple message of salvation that night; the first person to respond to give his heart to Jesus was Dr. Carl Butterfield! I have no delusions that it was my great preaching that touched his intellectual heart, nor my profound insights into

God's Word that brought him to that altar. It was the Proof-Producing God who showed Himself real to an unbelieving medical doctor in La Gonave, Haiti; a God of might and miracles who still works on behalf of His people whenever they will call on Him to do so.

When I had finished leading Carl in a prayer of repentance and commitment he said, "Pastor, we need to talk!"

"I'll bet we do!" I said, "Let me finish here at the altar and I'll meet you outside."

After I had finished praying with the others in the altar, I went outside to find Carl surrounded by several others of our missionary team rejoicing with him over his newfound faith in God.

"Pastor, you need to know that when we came on this trip I told you that I was a Catholic," Carl said. "The truth is that I was probably closer to being an agnostic; I seriously doubted that there was a real God. I had developed such a narrow set of parameters within which I would even accept the existence of a God. And, miraculously, He met me precisely within the envelope that I had defined. I saw two miracles today. I saw a woman give birth when it was anatomically impossible for her to do so; and I saw a baby born dead who came to life. I didn't even believe in miracles, but today I've seen two of them."

Suddenly an unexplainable thing happened. Without thinking, I heard words coming out of my mouth. "God's not finished yet, Carl; before the week is out you'll have your medical bag back!"

I couldn't believe my own words! Why would I have said such a dumb thing? God had already proven Himself to Carl and now I was going to blow it all with my rash statement. I kept trying to think of some way that I could back out of that statement, but nothing came to me. All I could do now was to pray fervently for God to back me up.

God had started our week of ministry with a day of miracles. The rest of the week was not marked with the same kind of dramatic works of God, but there were wonderful times of ministry nonetheless. Hundreds of people came daily to find someone who cared about their hurts and could minister to their suffering. We administered medical help to the limits of our ability and prayed for each of them.

Nightly we preached the Word of God and many responded to the message of God's love.

As the week drew to a close, we broke down our makeshift clinic, packed up our bags and headed back to Port au Prince for a day of rest before returning to the States. As soon as we reached the hotel in Petionville, the team headed for the swimming pool as I went to check our group into the hotel and get room assignments. I began filling out the paperwork and the desk clerk asked, "Pastor, is anyone in your group missing a piece of luggage?"

My heart jumped into my throat as I eagerly responded, "Yes, a medical bag about so big," (as I stretched my hands outward.)

"Would this be it?" he asked as he pointed toward Dr. Carl's medical bag on the floor. "We found this bag on the lawn in front of the hotel in the afternoon of the day you left for La Gonave. No one has any idea how it might have gotten there."

I picked up the bag and headed for the pool area. Our missionary team was really enjoying the cool water of the hotel pool and the noise level was quite high. I yelled across the pool area, "Dr. Carl Butterfield . . ."

"Yes?" came his reply in his jovial but most "doctoral" sounding voice.

"You remember your medical bag that was lost?" I asked, "Where would you like me to put it?"

His eyes widened, his mouth dropped open, and for a moment I halfway expected him to walk on water. Like a charging rhinoceros he plowed through the water of the pool creating a wake that would have shipwrecked the Queen Mary! When he regained his composure, he looked up at me standing on the side of the pool and said, "An impossible childbirth, a dead baby comes to life, and a lost bag is found. Three out of three is not bad, is it Pastor?" The words that I had spoken from a doubtful heart had proven to be prophetic and God had once more proven Himself to an agnostic doctor and a faithless pastor.

"Our Children and Grandchildren; 2004"

Chapter Eleven

A Romantic Night On The Terminal Floor

HOMELESS IN NEW YORK CITY!

Valentine's Day in 2007 is one of the most memorable nights that Joy and I have ever spent together! It all started when we received an invitation from missionary Larry Smith to come and teach for two weeks in Dhaka, Bangladesh. We also had a standing invitation from missionary Dwight Dobson in Colombo, Sri Lanka. In an effort to save on airfare, we usually tried to book two assignments back-to-back in the same part of the world. On this occasion, it required us to fly out of Jacksonville, Florida on the afternoon of February 14, Valentine's Day.

We arrived at the Jacksonville airport at noon under beautiful, sunny skies—another day in Paradise! We checked our bags at the counter and proceeded to the gate to await our plane's departure. So far, so good! A late winter blizzard had blown into the New England states that week and New York City was socked in with ice and snow. The air traffic system across America was in shambles as flight after flight was being cancelled in the Northeast. Just as we arrived at the boarding area, my Palm Pilot rang. I answered to the sound of a recorded message. "We regret to inform you that your flight to John F. Kennedy airport has been canceled due to weather conditions. We have taken the liberty to reschedule you on another flight to JFK via Atlanta. Please check with the nearest airline desk to confirm your reservations." This change was going to put us into JFK with very little time to make our connection to Dubai, in the United Arab Emirates.

We hurried back to the airline desk, concerned about our luggage which had already been checked on the canceled flight. The ticket agent sent us to the baggage area to have them find our baggage so we could check it onto the flight with us. After a few minutes of looking, the baggage handler emerged from the back with our familiar travel-weary luggage. Breathing a sigh of relief, we headed back to the ticket counter for the third time. The ticket agent changed our tickets for the flight to Atlanta, connecting with another flight to JFK and checked our luggage through to Dubai. She instructed us to pick up our luggage in Dubai and check it on through to Colombo, Sri Lanka, our final destination. Confident that our dilemma had been resolved, we headed for the boarding gate to board our flight to Atlanta.

After an uneventful flight to Atlanta, we landed and made our way to the boarding gate for the next leg of our flight to New York City. The ticket agent assured us that the flight had not been canceled and that we had nothing to worry about. We settled in to wait for the boarding call. After about ten minutes a voiced broke over the intercom, "Ladies and gentlemen, we regret to inform you that the flight to JFK has been canceled because of weather conditions. Please contact your nearest ticket agent to make other arrangements." Oh no! What do we do now?

We fought our way through the crowd to the front of the line and explained our dilemma to the ticket agent. She checked her computer and said,

"There are no more flights into JFK tonight, but we still have one more flight to LaGuardia leaving in 30 minutes."

"Can you get us on it?" I asked.

"Yes, but I'm not sure about your luggage," she said. We agreed for our luggage to take the next flight and we would retrieve it during our 14-hour layover in Dubai. We did not know then that we had seen our luggage for the last time; it was destined to disappear into the nether regions of "lost luggage land" somewhere in the bowels of the earth, never to be seen again.

After a windy, bumpy approach, we landed on the snow-covered runway of LaGuardia airport at about 11:30 p.m. that night. The shuttle to JFK had already shut down for the night. We took a $50 taxi ride from LaGuardia to JFK, praying that our connecting flight to Dubai had been delayed long enough for us get on board. But, such was not to be the case; as we arrived at the ticket counter we heard the crackle of the intercom, "Last boarding call for the

Emirates flight to Dubai; all passengers not at the boarding gate will not be allowed on board." I whipped out our tickets and hastily showed them to the agent. He shook his head and said, "You'll never make it sir; you won't even be able to clear the security area before the plane takes off! You'll have to take the next flight tomorrow morning!" We groaned and resigned ourselves to an overnight stay in New York City.

JFK airport is like a huge, self-contained city. You can find almost anything there. We found a hotel booking agency and started looking for a reasonably-priced hotel room. But, so did every other stranded traveler in this snowy blizzard that had gripped the transportation hub of the northeastern United States. The only hotel to be found was over an hour away and cost $250 for the night! Joy and I resigned ourselves to spending a romantic Valentine's night on the cold, concrete floor of the JFK terminal, along with hundreds of other stranded travelers.

We were awakened about 5:00 in the morning by a kindly policeman who apologetically told us that we would have to get up; the businesses were opening for the day and we were in the way. We found a bathroom, took a quick sponge bath and looked for a place to have breakfast. Not soon enough, we had our seat assignments and were waiting in the departure area for our 11:00 flight to Dubai.

For whatever reason, the flight to Dubai was not very heavily booked. There were plenty of seats, and Joy and I managed to each find three seats side by side. We raised the armrests and stretched out to catch up on some much-needed rest. By the time we reached Dubai, we were much more rested and in a somewhat better mood. We collected our carry-on luggage and deplaned into the beautiful, modern Dubai airport. Not really expecting to see our luggage, we nevertheless stopped by the baggage area to see if, by some miracle, it had made it onto the same flight with us. No such luck.

On our way to the boarding gate to spend the next 14 hours, we spotted a Dunkin' Donut shop! What a delightful surprise! We decided to throw our eternally-existent diet to the wind and have a couple of donuts and some coffee. I reached for my billfold, only to feel an empty spot where the familiar bulge usually was. Instantly, I realized exactly where my billfold was; it had fallen out of my pocket while I was lying down on the plane and was somewhere underneath the seats on the now-empty plane. I hurried back to the arrival gate, but the customs agents would not allow me through the clearing area. I was assured by the policeman that all lost and found items would be turned in to him and that he would hold the billfold for me. Yeah, right! You guessed it! Three credit cards, an ATM card, all my insurance cards, my driver's license, and $100 in cash were gone forever! I checked back with the policeman several times during the day, but the only thing turned in from the plane was an umbrella that someone had left. Fortunately, our passports, tickets and most of my cash were concealed on my person in a safe hiding place. My billfold had joined my luggage in that deep, dark hole in space!

I managed to find a telephone and called Dwight Dobson to let him know that we would be a day late in arriving in Sri Lanka. We settled in to spend a long day of waiting for our next flight to Colombo at 2:30 the next morning. We finally arrived in Sri Lanka at mid-morning on Saturday, three days after we left Jacksonville.

THE SRI LANKAN EXPERIENCE

Our normal routine is to prepare our teaching outlines and handouts weeks or months ahead of time. I then send them by e-mail to the missionary where they are translated into the local language. They are then e-mailed back to me, where I reformat them and prepare my PowerPoint slides and handouts in their final form. Then, I once more e-mail them back to the missionary to be printed and given to the students when they register for the course I will be teaching. It is a tried-and-true system that works well most of the time.

For some reason, the system broke down on the Sri Lanka trip. Whether it is the laid-back Sri Lankan culture, the "busy-ness" of the Bible College personnel, or a breakdown in communications, I do not know. What I do know is that I arrived on the scene with no translations in hand, no handouts ready for distribution, no printed teaching notes, no clothing to wear, and exhausted from the stress of what will surely go down as the worst airline trip in history (at least in our minds!) Needless to say, we were not happy campers in Colombo.

Missionary Dwight Dobson is a jaunty, jolly guy who never seems to be daunted by anything. I wanted very much to be angry with him for not getting my translations done in a timely manner. But, being angry with Dwight is like being angry with Santa Claus; you feel like the guilty one, instead of him. Despite ourselves, Joy and I fell instantly in love with Dwight and Anita, and we became fast friends. We spent a lot of time together in the next two weeks.

All my fears turned out to be groundless. Working behind the scenes, the Bible School personnel always managed to come through with the PowerPoint translations and the printed handouts just in the knick of time, sometimes even at the last minute, just as I was about to begin the class with prayer.

In the Sri Lankan culture, "loss of face" is a big thing. They are deeply fearful of being embarrassed. I did not know this, and I could not understand why my students were not responding to my direct questions in class. Try as I might, I could not get them to open up in class. They sat there like respectful, but speechless zombies, not responding to anything I said or did. I usually don't have much trouble evoking some kind of response from students, so I was really perplexed over this turn of events. Dwight explained to me that they were listening and absorbing what I was saying, but that they were afraid to answer questions lest they be wrong. They were afraid to be embarrassed.

So, unbeknownst to Joy, I decided to try a new tactic with the class. She was as concerned as I was that the students were not responding, so the next time I asked a question, she decided to venture her own opinion to break the ice. I purposely took the opposite (and wrong) position from her. She and I began to argue a theological point in front of the class. They were amused and intrigued to see us disagreeing with each other in the class. Soon, I began to see hands raised as they wanted to chime in on the issue being discussed. Some of them agreed with Joy's position, and some of them agreed with my incorrect position. They may have gone away with mixed feelings about that subject, but from that day on we did not have any more problems with getting responses in class.

The Sri Lankan students were a beautiful and gracious people, and in the two weeks that we were there they captured our hearts. We fell in love with those young people and by the time we left Colombo, we felt that our family of spiritual offspring had grown considerably. I'm sure we will be back!

BANGLADESH

(Bangladesh is a politically sensitive area of the world. To avoid unpleasant and dangerous repercussions, the names in the following story have been changed. God knows who these people are and He will reward them with a hero's welcome when we get home!)

After an overnight flight from Sri Lanka, our missionary host met us at the Dhaka airport on Friday morning. He is a phenomenal man—a true apostle to Bangladesh. On the strength of his vision and the power of God, he has made a powerful impact upon the crowded nation of Bangladesh. After a few hours of rest, he took us to see the largest of the many schools and orphanages that he has started in this needy country. The many miraculous stories of how this came about are far too numerous to try to cover in this narrative. After hosting us for the day, he turned us over to his trusted sidekick, flew off to one of the many conferences he has to attend, and then on the States to be there for the birth of his grandchild. That, of course, takes priority over everything! (Coming from a grandfather of 11!)

Bangladesh is one of the most populated countries in the world. Imagine a country half the size of the Florida peninsula, with half the population of the United States in that one tiny area. That's Bangladesh! The population is 85% Muslim with only about 3% Christians, and that includes Catholics, Protestants and cults! The rest of the population is divided between the Hindus and Buddhists. It is illegal to proselytize Muslims in Bangladesh and a person can be hanged for converting someone to Christianity. We were taking our lives into our own hands by even being there doing the work of God.

The organization that sponsored our teaching mission to Bangladesh has quite a large presence in the country with over 400 churches! Even so, it has hardly made a dent in the bustling population of this tiny country. The denomination has a multi-story headquarters building in Dhaka that houses a local church, a

Christian school, a media center that produces radio and television programs, the administrative offices for the denomination, and a Bible school that trains workers in the Kingdom of God. It was to this Bible school that we had been invited to come and teach.

We had been instructed not to prepare our usual curriculum for this assignment. We were told only that the students would receive a manual entitled "Who Is Jesus?" We did not even receive a copy of the manual; so, when we arrived on the scene we had no idea what we would be doing. Both of us are very structured individuals, so you can imagine how uncomfortable we were with this assignment. We were told on Sunday afternoon that we would be teaching 91 college-age students who knew little, if anything about Jesus or Christianity. The administration of the Bible College had discovered that there was such a hunger for higher education among the young people of Bangladesh that they would even apply to a Christian Bible College just so they could get a college degree. They held a two-week orientation seminar for prospective students who wanted to know more about the college. At the end of the two weeks, after finding out what the Bible College was all about, if they still wanted to attend they were accepted as students. What had started out as a recruiting tool for the college had turned into a very effective evangelistic outreach! And, because of a loophole in the Bengali law, we were not even doing anything illegal. According to their law, it is acceptable to answer the questions of anyone who wants to know more about your religion. Ninety-one young people had come to us wanting to know more about Christianity. What a fertile field in which to labor!

All of our previous assignments involved teaching people who were already saved and already involved in ministry or preparing to go into the ministry. Never before had I faced a challenge such as this one. Where do you begin with people who have never even heard of God? Who have no idea of creation, sin or salvation? Our work was cut out for us! However, I've always liked an exciting challenge, so we dived right into preparation to teach for the coming week. I was to start teaching on Tuesday morning and it was already Sunday afternoon; so, the real challenge was to prepare my lesson plans, get my PowerPoint slides translated, and get the student's fill-in-the-blank outlines printed before class each day. One of the staff translators was assigned to me and I kept him busy for the next 10 days.

The first lesson was, "How Did It All Begin?" I presented two alternatives, Creation and Evolution. One of the benefits of doing a Master's level program in the behavioral sciences at a secular university was that I am well-versed in the theory of evolution. I know about evolution from the perspective of a secularist as well as a Christian believer. I gave equal time to each view and then asked the students to choose which view was the logical view. It was interesting that, having never been exposed to either view, without exception these students chose creationism as the more logical explanation for how we came into existence. I make no claim that I presented the two views with no personal bias; however, I am certain that I had less bias than most secular professors who present evolution as a scientific fact and creationism as a superstitious fairy tale.

In the next six days, I took the students from creationism to Adam and Eve, the fall of man, the existence of evil, God's plan of redemption, man's right to make moral choices, to how to become a child of God. I purposely avoided "religious" words like "Christian" and "saved," and used words like "choosing Jesus" and "making Jesus Lord of your life." As the week came to an end, the vast majority of the students had accepted Jesus as Lord and had become genuine believers. Considering that 85% of them were Muslims, this was quite a victory!

The real challenge came one week later when I taught them about the abiding presence of the Holy Spirit in the believer's life. In our Pentecostal theology, the infilling of the Holy Spirit is a uniquely supernatural experience involving the spiritual gift of speaking in tongues. It is something that cannot be taught, it must simply be experienced. Would these neophyte Christians have the faith to believe for such a spectacular miracle? On Tuesday morning I taught about "The Work Of The Holy Spirit In The Believer's Life" and I gave them nine reasons why they should be filled with the Holy Spirit. That evening, I taught them how to receive the Holy Spirit. To avoid the awkwardness of working around the altar with an interpreter, I asked the president of the college to pray with the students to receive the Holy Spirit. At the appropriate time, I turned the service to him and I stepped aside.

Quite a number of the students had come forward to receive the Holy Spirit at the invitation. One particular young man had his hands raised and appeared to be really responding to the presence of God. Although I could speak no Bangla, I went over to lay hands on him and pray with him. I was conscious of the fact that God appeared to be moving in other areas of the room, but most of my attention was focused on this one young man. As I was praying for him, the president slipped up behind me and whispered to me, "They are falling out on the floor in the back of the room!" I had said nothing to them about being "slain in the Spirit" or overcome by the presence of God, so I was somewhat intrigued by what the president has told me.

As soon as possible, I left the young man praying at the front of the room and went back to see what was happening. There, on the floor, lying side-by-side were four young men, three with hands raised praying in tongues and a fourth lying as still as a dead man, totally out under the power of God. I stood there thrilled and amused, chuckling to myself in wonderment at such an awesome God, when suddenly one of the young men praying in tongues began praying in English! And, his English was without any accent at all! This was not the first time I had heard someone speak in an identifiable language when the Holy Spirit came upon them, but it is still a source of amazement to me every time it happens. When I got back to the front of the room, the young man I had first prayed with was now on the floor speaking with tongues. Next to him lay another young man, totally oblivious to anyone else around him, worshiping God in the Holy of Holies! A flash of movement caught my right eye and I turned in time to see a young lady speaking in tongues and falling out under the power of the Holy Spirit. What made all these manifestations so noteworthy was that these students had never seen anything like this. I had said nothing in my lesson about physical responses to the power of the Holy Spirit. There was no "stage setting" here, no mass hysteria, no power of suggestion, and nobody pushing them down. These were sovereign acts of a mighty God who chose to bless these hungry young people with a manifestation of His mighty power. Hallelujah!

We encountered more Satanic attacks on this trip than any we have ever taken. From canceled flights, to lost luggage, to my lost billfold, it soon became evident that Satan was trying to keep us from making this trip. He even afflicted Joy with "traveler's sickness" and confined her to our apartment, never very far from the bathroom. He also afflicted me with an attack of Giardia, an intestinal parasite that manifests itself with extreme weakness. I even had to stop teaching in mid-class one morning because I could no longer stand up. I handed my notes to the interpreter and asked him to finish teaching the class. Because of what I perceived to be the missionary's failure to adequately inform me of what my assignment was, I fought a two-week battle with my attitude, although bad attitude is not usually a problem for me. However, despite all these vicious attacks of the enemy, Father God came through and we experienced a wonderful victory. The sight of all those young people praying through to the infilling of the Holy Spirit made it all worth while!

Chapter Twelve

Walking In The Footsteps Of Paul

"Backpacking in the footsteps of the Apostle Paul"

It was 5:00 in the morning as we watched the big bus pull away leaving us in a cloud of diesel smoke. Three miles from the ancient ruins of Ephesus, here we stood on the side of the road, before daybreak, not knowing a soul, in what we thought to be a country hostile to Americans. Expecting at any minute for some terrorist with a crescent-shaped knife to come out of the shadows and slice our throats, we thought surely we were destined to be on CNN the next day. Suddenly, out of the shadows, there stepped…an ANGEL????

But, wait; I'm getting way ahead of my story. It all started when Joy and I decided that we would like to film a documentary about all the cities in which Paul built churches around the Aegean

Sea. It would make an interesting addition to our classes on the Pauline Epistles. We would pack everything we needed in two backpacks and just go wherever our fancy took us, just like two college kids on summer break. Browsing the Internet, we found the "Balkan Senior Flexipass" which allows you to ride on any train in the Balkans, "hop on, hop off" style. We bought one for each of us. Our first big mistake was not realizing how big an area the Balkans covers. We boarded our train in Vienna at 3:00 Sunday afternoon; on Monday afternoon at 5:30 we pulled into the station at Skopia, Macedonia, where we were met by missionary Eddie White. After a day and a half visiting with the Whites and the Whitmans we boarded the train for Thessaloniki, 2nd largest city in Greece and the city to which Paul wrote the Epistles to the Thessalonians. The modern city is built over the site of the ancient city, so there isn't much to see in the way of ruins. It was just the idea that we were walking the very streets that the Apostle Paul walked. The Via Egnatia is the main street (as it was in Paul's day. It's a large, paved boulevard today, lined with skyscrapers and businesses; but it's the same street, in the same location.)

    The next morning we strapped on our backpacks and boarded the train for the Greek town of Drama, the nearest town to the ancient ruins of Philippi. From the train station in Drama, we walked to a hotel and checked in. We found a bus going by the ruins and bought our tickets. 15 minutes later we were standing beside the ruins of Philippi. My heart was pounding as we gazed at the first ruins we had actually seen. Philippi was the site where the first European convert to Christianity was made (Lydia, the seller of purple, 20 years after Christ's resurrection) and the first Christian church in Europe. Paul and his band (Timothy, Titus, & Luke) all visited here. It may even have been Luke's home town. The Via Egnatia connected Philippi with the distant city of Thessalonica.

    The next morning, feeling very satisfied with our trip so far, we boarded the train for Istanbul, Turkey. What we didn't know was that the Turks and the Greeks were once at war with each other and there still is a little bad blood between them. When we got to the border, the customs agents boarded the train and herded us off onto a platform with a station house that looked like a stagecoach way station out of the Wild, Wild West. One of the agents came by yelling "Passaports, passaports!" It looked like he had an armful, so I gave him ours as well. The train pulled away and left us standing on the siding. Hmmm!

After about 4 hours, word filtered down to us that the Turkish Railway system was sending a train for us. All I can say is that if you're thinking about riding a Turkish train…DON'T! Think about having to potty through a 4-inch hole in the floor on a train rocking and rolling along at 80 mph over an antiquated rail system, with no toilet tissue! GET THE PICTURE??? Not a pretty sight! We arrived in Istanbul (formerly known as Constantinople) about midnight, 4 hours late. We caught a taxi and headed for our youth hostel where we already had reservations. Yup! They had rented our room when we didn't show up on time. Fortunately, the owners also owned a hotel next door and they were able to put us in there for the night.

Istanbul has no biblical significance, so we had no interest in sightseeing there. The next morning we caught a taxi and headed for the bus terminal (we had given up on the Turkish train system!) Our helpful taxi driver (beware of "helpful" taxi drivers) advised us that the bus to Ephesus was full and the next one would run the next day. I saw a sign that advertised a flight to where we wanted to go for only 89 million lira (about $60) so we decided to fly. After shelling out 60 million lira ($40) to our "helpful" taxi driver, we went into the terminal only to discover that there were no flights leaving that day. So we boarded another taxi for a trip to the ferry terminal (this driver only charged us $10 for the same trip!) At the terminal we discovered that the ferry was full and the next one would run the next day! Grrrrr! I bit my tongue to keep from venting my frustration on the poor ticket agent. "Well, do you have two tickets to ANYWHERE? I just want to get out of Istanbul." In an hour we were on a ferry to Yalova, a town I had never heard of on the south side of the Sea of Marmara. Thirty minutes later we were asking a policeman where the bus terminal was in Yalova. He pointed right next door to the ferry terminal and we walked over. "Bus to Selcuk?" I said to the ticket agent as simply as I could, so as not to be misunderstood. He said something to me in Turkish and waited for my reply. I guess he saw the blank look on my face; he wrote down 23:30 on a slip of paper and pushed it across the counter at me.

I asked when it would arrive in Selcuk and he wrote 07:00 on the paper. I nodded my head and bought two tickets for the overnight ride to Selcuk. The bus seats reclined and it was a very comfortable ride. We both slept surprisingly well. However, we made better time than the ticket agent had anticipated. At 5:00 a.m. the driver tapped me on the shoulder to awaken me and said, "Selcuk!" and pointed outside. I looked at my watch and couldn't believe we were already there. I protested that we were too early at our destination, but the driver just shrugged his shoulders. By now, the commotion had awakened the other passengers and they were glaring at us as if to say, "Out! Yankee intruders, so we can be on our way!" We hefted our backpacks onto our shoulders, got off the bus into the murky darkness and watched them drive off down the lonely road into the distance, leaving us standing in the darkness, somewhere in Turkey on the side of a lonely road. (See the opening paragraph at the beginning of this chapter.)

The leathery-skinned woman standing before us in the pre-dawn hours sure didn't look much like an angel, but I'm convinced that she was. Why else would she have been there at that time of the morning?

"Do you need a place to stay?" she said, in flawless English. Not yet sure what she was up to, I hesitatingly said,

"Well, as a matter of fact, we do!"

"I have five guest rooms in my home…very clean…very comfortable. You can stay there if you like," she said.

"How much?" I suspiciously asked. Thinking for a moment, she said,

"20 million liras." I was wondering what kind of a room she could have for $13.

"Can we see your rooms?" I asked.

"Certainly," she replied. We got in her car and headed for her home. The rooms were spacious and clean and the beds were very inviting. We took the room and settled in to sleep through the rest of the pre-dawn hours. She fed us a great breakfast and then called her nephew to drive us to the ruins of ancient Ephesus and arranged to pick us up four hours later.

The ruins of Ephesus defy description. By far the best preserved ruins of any biblical site, the city stretches over many acres of land. The Apostle Paul loved the city of Ephesus. He spent at least 3 years of his life here, using it as a base of operations while he ministered throughout the Aegean crescent. It was from Ephesus that he wrote his epistles to the Corinthians. And it was the church in Ephesus to which Paul wrote the classic Epistle to the Ephesians. The ruins of Ephesus are dominated by the façade of a huge, 3-story library which housed the literary collection of Paul's day. It is a massive structure that has withstood numerous earthquakes down through the centuries. Church history tells us that John the Apostle took Jesus' command from the cross very seriously, and adopted Jesus' mother Mary as his own mother. He moved her to the seaside city of Ephesus where she lived out her life. There is a site there that is reputed to be Mary's home during the final days of her life. The Roman Catholic Church has researched the site and declared it to be authentic. After his release from the Isle of Patmos, John also lived out his life in the city of Ephesus.

Shukran (our Selcuk angel) fed us an excellent supper meal and we spent the next night in her guest room as well. When we checked out the next morning, I asked her how much we owed her. She thought for a minute, lifted her nose in the air as if to engage in a bargaining battle, and then said, "50 million lira!" I quickly calculated that to be about $33 for 2 nights, 4 meals, and a taxi service. Although haggling over price is the accepted mode of trade in Turkey, I gladly paid her what she asked, with no haggling (can you believe that this "king of the tightwads" actually did that?)

We boarded the ferry headed for the Greek island of Patmos, where the Apostle John spent his exile years and from which he wrote the book of Revelation. Were it not for the beautiful village which the Greeks have built in the harbor, Patmos would be a barren, bleak environment. Our intention was to spend the afternoon sightseeing on Patmos, then board the ferry for Athens at 2:00 the next morning. We ended up sleeping on the padded seats in the booth of a restaurant at the ferry terminal. Our boat finally arrived at 6:00 a.m., 4 hours late. By now, however, we had become accustomed to the lack of punctuality. That seems to be an American thing, anyhow!

About mid-afternoon we arrived in the port city of Piraeus (the port of Athens) and checked into a fairly nice hotel 2 blocks from the terminal, where we spent the next 2 nights. That evening we visited the Parthenon and Mars Hill, where Paul preached his sermon to the Athenians. It is significant to note that Athens was the only major city in the area in which Paul did not establish a church.

The next day we spent at the ruins of Corinth (today known as Korinthos.) At the time of Paul's stay there, the city probably numbered a half-million inhabitants. It was the New York City of its day, the crossroads of commerce and culture in that part of the world. It was a church birthed out of paganism and plagued with immaturity. Paul had to confront a lot of problems in this immature church. What they did have was influence; the church grew and prospered and made a significant impact on that area of the world. Our trip was coming to a close and we were ready to be home. We debated flying from Athens, but the airfare was exorbitant. And besides, our train passes were already paid for. We would just enjoy our leisurely, 2-day train ride back to Vienna, our temporary home. That morning we boarded the most beautiful train we have ever ridden on! In preparation for the upcoming Olympics, the Greeks bought a brand-new train for the Athens-Thessaloniki route. It was first-class all the way. Royalty treatment in the dining car, fully reclining seats, and a breathtakingly beautiful ride through the Greek mountains; what more could you ask for?

Then, the other shoe fell! We were to change trains at Thessaloniki for the train that would take us to Vienna. When I went to confirm our reservations, the ticket agent informed me that there was a rail strike in Skopia and that no trains would be allowed through there for an indefinite period of time. After exhausting all other possibilities for re-routing, we finally had to buy airline tickets to Salzburg, Austria and take a 4-hour train ride home to Vienna. We arrived in Vienna at 6:08 Friday morning, exhausted and exhilarated, but glad to be home. We did, however, discover why 65-year olds don't go backpacking; it will kill you! Everybody ought to do it once; just do it before you're 30 years old! "So, what's the big deal!" you may ask, "Paul did it with no modern transportation." True, but Paul had a lifetime to do it in; we did it in 10 days!

Chapter Thirteen

The Closing Chapter

Somewhere around my sixtieth birthday a horrifying thought occurred to me. I'm coming to the last chapter of my life. I've made so many mistakes in my life; I've learned so much from my failures and the few successes that God has helped me to achieve in life. It would be a shame to take all those lessons to the grave with me and for no one else to benefit from them. It was as if the Father was urging me to pass those lessons on to the next generation so they wouldn't have to make the same mistakes. After all, it is a wise man that benefits from his own mistakes; but, it is a brilliant man who learns a lesson from someone else's mistakes. Although it had been twenty-five years since I had felt those feelings, I began to feel that my ministry at the First Assembly of God in Gainesville was coming to an end and the final chapter of my life was about to begin.

In 1979 I had a distinct purpose for pursuing my Master's degree at Assemblies of God Theological Seminary (AGTS.) I wanted to enhance my ministry in Gainesville and to gain more tools to help me achieve my ministry goals. In 1989, however, my reasons for pursuing my doctoral degree from Erskine Seminary were not nearly so clearly defined. I already had a lively, growing church and was secure in my position as pastor. I really didn't need a doctoral degree, and I didn't relish the idea of going back to school at age 50. However, when the opportunity to enroll in the extension program at Erskine presented itself, it just seemed like it was the right thing to do. I didn't know it then, but God was preparing me for the last chapter of my life.

That was not, however, the only preparation God was doing. In 1991 a young, 19-year old freshman named Michael Patz arrived in Gainesville to attend the University of Florida. On his first Saturday in town he was driving around to familiarize himself with the city. When he passed by the First Assembly of God, he turned into the vacant parking lot. He pulled under the shade of a tree and got out to walk around. Although he had never accepted Christ as his savior, he had been in church enough to recognize the presence of God. Suddenly, there on the parking lot he was overcome with his "lostness" and the fact that he was not ready for heaven or, indeed, even for life. There, underneath a tree, with no one but the Holy Spirit to help him, he invited Jesus to come into his heart. The next morning he showed up for church. He asked someone to point him to the youth pastor. "My name is Mike Patz," he said, "and I gave my heart to Jesus yesterday in your parking lot. I need someone to disciple me!" Our youth pastor took Mike under his wing and nurtured this newborn child of God.

A year later our youth pastor resigned to pursue a different career path. He came to me with what I thought was a ridiculous suggestion.

"When you look for someone to take my place, Pastor," he said, "I'd like to recommend Mike Patz."

"Are you crazy, Alan?" I said, "He has absolutely no qualifications to be a youth pastor! He is a baby Christian; he has no ministerial credentials, no training in youth ministry, and no experience. Why in the world would I want him for a youth pastor?"

"Trust me on this, Pastor," Alan said, "if you don't do this you will be cheating yourself and these young people; Mike has what it takes to become a great youth pastor." Alan had earned some credibility with me so I reluctantly decided to give Mike a chance. He had not earned the title of Youth Pastor, however; so, I gave him the title of Youth Leader.

Mike hit the ground with both feet running; he was a fireball of energy. He began going to the high schools at lunch and eating with the students. He organized groups to meet and pray around the flagpole. He shared the lives of our teenagers and they fell head over heels in love with him. But, most of all, he preached the Word. Mike's gospel was a no-nonsense gospel. He expected his young people not only to talk the talk but to walk the walk. He cut them no slack when it came to serving God; it was all or nothing. The youth group grew, and grew, and grew some more.

Meanwhile, in addition to his studies at the university, Mike enrolled in the Berean College ministerial training program through the Assemblies of God. In time, he completed all 33 of the courses required and received his credentials as an Assemblies of God minister. He fell in love with, and subsequently married Ruth, one of the beautiful, young Hispanic girls in our congregation. Meanwhile, our church fell more and more in love with Mike and his growing family.

In time, I promoted Mike to the role of Associate Pastor and gave him the responsibility of finding his replacement for the youth department. As with everything else he had done, Mike became an excellent right-hand man for me. He was teachable, energetic, self-motivated, and not cowed or intimidated by my strong leadership style. We worked well together and he became my Timothy in the Lord. When God began to deal with me about the last phase of my ministry I called Mike into my office one day.

"It won't be real soon," I said, "but, I believe God is getting me ready for a new chapter of my life and it will mean my stepping down as Senior Pastor of First Assembly. I would like for you to pray about being my replacement."

"But, Pastor, I don't see myself as a pastor," he said, "I've always thought of myself as a missionary; I'm not sure I want to be a pastor!"

"Well Mike," I replied, "I'm a missionary; I travel and teach abroad frequently, and with the church's blessing. This is a missionary church and they will want a missionary pastor." When he left my office I knew I had not convinced him and that God was going to have to do the convincing. It took almost a year of the Holy Spirit's prompting and convincing before Mike walked into my office one day to announce,

"Pastor, I believe that God has shown me that Gainesville is to be my home and I'm ready to talk about becoming the Senior Pastor."

In the Assemblies of God the congregation has the final say in who is to be their pastor. In fact, it is usually considered poor protocol for the outgoing pastor to try to influence the selection of a new pastor. But, I had invested a quarter of a century in First Assembly! This was my family; and, when I stepped down this would still be my home church. I wasn't about to turn my back as though I had no interest in who was to become my pastor. I didn't care about protocol; I loved my congregation too much to just walk away!

I've always had a deep respect for our constitutional form of church government however; I knew that the people needed to be included in this crucial decision. My first step was to take the matter to the church board. They enthusiastically endorsed Mike to be the next Senior Pastor of First Assembly. I purposely "leaked" the news to the congregation that I was grooming Pastor Mike to be their next Senior Pastor. The following year at the annual business meeting, I presented his name to the congregation and requested that they ratify him as their Senior Pastor upon my resignation. Not surprisingly, they gave him a near-unanimous vote of approval.

In April, 2004, at the end of 25 years of ministry of the First Assembly of God in Gainesville, Joy and I turned the reins of leadership over to Mike and Ruthie Patz. We left immediately for Vienna, Austria to begin the next chapter in our ministry.

Our ministry today involves raising up pastoral leadership in nations around the world. We believe that the most effective missionary evangelism is not for Americans to try to reach people groups with the message of God's love, but for us to raise up and equip leaders within their own cultures to reach their own people for God. We try to teach pastors and aspiring pastors how to be more effective in reaching their cultures with the message of God's love. To date, we have visited in over 80 countries of the world and have taught pastor's classes in over 20 of those countries.

The rigors of trans-oceanic travel can be exhausting. Airport ticket counters and waiting areas lose their glamour pretty quickly. Sixteen hour plane rides take their toll on anyone, but they are especially tiring to a couple of senior citizens. People often ask us, "How long will you keep this up?" There is only one answer we can give them. Jesus only made one prayer request. He said, "Pray ye therefore the Lord of the harvest, that he will send forth laborers into his harvest." (Matthew 9:38) We have seen the ripened harvest, and we know the laborers are few. We're doing our best to fulfill our Lord's prayer request. As long as He provides us the strength and the wherewithal to get the job done, there is no end in sight. The harvest is still waiting!

CPSIA information can be obtained at www.ICGtesting.com
Printed in the USA
LVOW061248020612

284316LV00004B/3/P